THE GREAT GAME

THE GREAT GAME

THE MYTH AND REALITY OF ESPIONAGE

Frederick P. Hitz

ALFRED A. KNOPF

NEW YORK

2004

THIS IS A BORZOI BOOK
PUBLISHED BY ALFRED A. KNOPF

Library of Congress Cataloging-in-Publication Data
Hitz, Frederick Porter, [date]
The great game / Frederick P. Hitz.—1st ed.
p.   cm.
ISBN 0-375-41210-7
1. Spy stories, English—History and criticism.   2. Spy stories,
American—History and criticism.   3. United States.
Central Intelligence Agency.   4. Hitz, Frederick Porter, 1939–.
5. Espionage, American.   6. Espionage.   I. Title.
PR830.S65H57 2004
823'.087209—dc21   2003054507

Manufactured in the United States of America
First Edition

To
Mary Buford
and Eliza,
the only women
in my life

Contents

THE GREAT GAME

Introduction

> When he comes to the Great Game he must go
> alone—alone, and at peril of his head. . . . From
> time to time, God causes men to be born—and thou
> art one of them—who have a lust to go abroad at the
> risk of their lives and discover news—today it may
> be of far-off things, tomorrow of some hidden
> mountain, and the next day of some near-by men
> who have done a foolishness against the State. These
> souls are very few; and of these few, not more than
> ten are of the best. . . . We of the Game are beyond
> protection. If we die, we die. Our names are blotted
> from the book. . . . When everyone is dead the Great
> Game is finished. Not before.[1]

This is a book about the Great Game—espionage, or spying.

Kim Philby, who knew something about the subject, defined espionage as the collection of "secret information from foreign countries by illegal means."[2] That strikes me as a useful definition.

The information collected must be "secret," or protected by its owner from disclosure in the normal course of events.

The information itself must have some strategic significance. As Sherman Kent, one of the founders of the Board of National

3

Estimates at the CIA, once wrote, it ought to be information requiring "action" by policy makers.[3]

The information must come from "foreign countries." We are not talking about domestic snooping.

Finally, the information must be acquired by "illegal means." The owner or creator of the information does not want to give it up. It has to be stolen.

In the popular mind, espionage most often connotes *human source intelligence,* or HUMINT, in the bafflegab of the spy bureaucracies. In other words, it is information obtained from human agents, or spies, usually under an arrangement in which the agents participate wittingly or willingly.

In the United States, espionage has often entailed a mixture of the technical and the human. In this we took our lead from the British. We were introduced to the mysteries of *signals intelligence,* or SIGINT, in World War I with the interception of the Zimmermann telegram by the British Secret Intelligence Service in 1917, and the incident helped bring us into the war. In the 1920s, with Herbert O. Yardley's "Black Chamber" in the State Department, the United States successfully read Japanese naval telegrams and was thus able to monitor the buildup of the Japanese fleet.

The crowning achievements in this early era came about when the British acquired replicas of the German Enigma code machine in 1939, through Polish intermediaries. The spectacular success at decryption that then took place at Bletchley Park enabled the British and the Americans to read German diplomatic and military signals traffic during World War II. The United States soon followed by cracking the Japanese naval code leading to a successful interdiction of the Japanese fleet in the Battle of Midway in 1942. SIGINT cooperation between the United Kingdom and the United States continued after the war and led to some of the most spectacular espionage successes of the Cold War.

In addition, the United States developed some remarkable technical capabilities on its own in the mid-1950s with the U-2 overhead reconnaissance aircraft. Later the Corona satellite program succeeded in photographing Soviet missile test sites and indeed every inch of Soviet territory over time.

Covert action (CA), or what the British term special operations, largely involves human agents, but it is action-oriented as opposed to information-oriented. Covert action may be as simple as disseminating unattributable or *black* propaganda, or as big and complex as coup plotting, assassination planning, sabotage, or waging guerrilla war. The principal feature that distinguishes covert action is that the hand of the perpetrator is intended *not* to show. U.S. intelligence invented the seemingly benign term "plausible deniability."

In spy fiction, by contrast, there is little distinction drawn between operations designed purely for the production of intelligence information (classic espionage) and those mounted to produce a physical result (covert action). As we shall observe, the human qualities and spy tradecraft which bring about success in classic espionage operations are often at war with the boldness and manipulative techniques needed for a successful covert action operation—and where the same people are called upon to do both, there is often a conflict in disciplines, sometimes leading to systemic malfunction. By definition, spy operations to collect intelligence information are designed to be carried out clandestinely and often over a long time period. Their very success depends upon maintaining secrecy. Iraq is never to know if the CIA penetrated Saddam's inner circle. By contrast, covert action is intended to produce a visible outcome. Only its true sponsorship is intended to remain a secret.

Finally, the collection of secret information from foreign countries by illegal means presupposes that nations that do not wish their secrets to be stolen will seek to combat the theft—by *counterintelligence* (CI). "Counterintelligence" refers both to the efforts made to protect one's own secrets *and* to the measures taken to penetrate a rival intelligence service to learn its secrets. Many of the great fictional spy stories are in fact tales of counterintelligence.

This book arises out of an eponymous freshman seminar that I have been teaching in recent years at Princeton University. In the seminar, great works of spy fiction are compared to actual espionage operations. In the course of this seminar, my students and I have concluded that if one leaves the more fantastic conceits of Ian Fleming and Tom Clancy aside, real espionage cases are often *more* bizarre, *more* deserving of a place in Ripley's than the fictional accounts.

Although spying is often referred to as the second-oldest profession, the spy novel as a distinct literary genre dates only from the late nineteenth century. I thus start my seminar with Rudyard Kipling's *Kim,* which depicts espionage in defense of empire, the "Great Game." This term of course refers to the competition among Britain, France, and czarist Russia for control of the Hindu Kush, and the area now encompassed by the modern states of Afghanistan, Pakistan, and much of India. In *Kim* and the other early spy novels such as Erskine Childers's *The Riddle of the Sands* and John Buchan's *The Thirty-nine Steps,* the *spy* is the protagonist. He is the man on the ground who does the dirty work, and the novel is about his adventures. Later, as the genre matures, the focus shifts. We learn more about the organizations created to run or catch spies and focus less on the spy as hero. The hero, if there is one, is the case officer or spy runner who is managing or pursuing the spy.

The methodology here is to isolate the prominent elements of espionage operations, beginning where any consideration of this subject ought to start—with the recruitment of spies—and observe first how the subject is treated in the spy literature.

After reviewing several celebrated fictional accounts of the phenomenon being discussed, I turn to the real thing and analyze the particulars of actual cases. It will be left to the reader to decide whether the truth about espionage is stranger than fiction. I break cover only in the epilogue, giving you my view and the reasons therefor.

The subject of espionage is itself endlessly fascinating, because it deals with the rawest, most elemental side of human behavior. People have been intrigued by the essence of spying since Judas betrayed Jesus with a kiss for thirty pieces of silver in the garden of Gethsemane. Why did he do it? For the money? Out of envy? To obtain power? For revenge? What is peculiar about the act of betrayal? What human qualities are involved? How does one get a Judas to work for one's own cause?

In the pages ahead, may the reader discern the answers to some of these questions.

One

Recruitment

To be blunt, leadership is the ability to dominate and get your way. To do that requires the ability to inspire and provide trust, self-confidence, recognizable professional skills, caring, and many other qualities.

I submit you need these same skills when recruiting an agent, whose cooperation with you, if exposed, holds risk of death, imprisonment, or at a minimum dishonor. As you move into the recruitment "pitch" and the full dimensions of what you are asking dawns on the prospective agent, he or she looks at you with consummate disbelief, even when he or she more or less expects something is coming. Although perhaps not articulated, their eyes scream that what you want is the most ludicrous thing ever requested of them. In the end you succeed through leadership, for through the development of the agent you have brought yourself into a position of dominance and trust.[1]

This excerpt from Duane "Dewey" Clarridge's autobiography is an experienced spy runner's take on the qualities needed to effect recruitment of an agent. In order to collect secret information from foreign countries, which is the essence of spying, one must recruit human sources to gain access to that information. Clarridge has described the straight-up recruitment approach, at which he was adept, but that approach is obviously not the only way to acquire the keys to the secret kingdom. There are as many possibilities as there are human foibles and motivations to exploit. In the textbook case, recruitment occurs only after the potential spy has been identified as having access to the information being sought, has been assessed as vulnerable to a recruitment approach, and has been cultivated to bring him into a state of mind where he might consider a recruitment pitch without denouncing the recruiter to the authorities. The object of the recruitment pitch is to acquire control over the prospective spy so that he will accept direction from the spy runner.

Seldom does the saga unfold in the manner prescribed in the Sarratt (the British Secret Intelligence Service, known as SIS or MI6) or CIA training manuals. A good fictional illustration of this is contained in David Ignatius's account of agent operations in the Middle East, *Agents of Innocence*. The central character, CIA case officer Tom Rogers (who is loosely modeled on a real CIA officer killed in the Beirut embassy bombing in 1983), cultivates the deputy chief of Fatah intelligence as a secret informant on terrorist threats to U.S. citizens traveling and working in Lebanon, Saudi Arabia, and Egypt. Rogers is an experienced Arabist with good Arabic-language skills who painstakingly establishes rapport with PECOCK, as the Fatah official is encrypted. (A recruited or potential spy is given a cryptonym in order to protect his identity in normal correspondence between the field and Headquarters.) Rogers's recruitment philosophy is remarkably uncomplicated. It is based on the simple observation that people like to talk: old politicians want to tell war stories and young revolutionaries want to explain how they plan to change the world. Rogers observes that they should not be telling him these things but they always do. All of them, all over the world, seek the ear of an interested American, he believes, and with his open, straightforward approach, just listening beats all the gadgets and formal contractual procedures for obtaining useful secret information.

> Recruiting someone is about getting him to do what you want, rather than just forcing him to do what he doesn't want. I learned a long time ago that it's easy to manipulate people—if you know what *you* want from them and don't tell them why you're being so friendly.[2]

Rogers's superiors do not share his philosophy. In order to secure PECOCK's cooperation as a penetration of Fatah, they want a more businesslike arrangement in which control is exchanged for money. When Rogers is unsuccessful in getting PECOCK to plant a bug in the conference room of a rival Palestinian terrorist organization, the recruitment issue comes to a head:

> In the world of recruiting agents, playing by the book meant contracts that were clearly understood by both sides, ones that imposed on the slippery and deceitful world of espionage, some of the order of the legal world. Marsh liked relationships that were clear and straightforward. I buy your services for an agreed-upon price; you agree to deliver certain material in exchange; we both profit by the relationship. He understood that sort of arrangement, and he believed in it. Each side knew the risks and rewards. It was a transaction between adults. What troubled Marsh were relationships that were more complicated, where subtler and less orderly moti-

vations prevailed. Those relationships—based on frail human emotions like friendship, respect, and loyalty—were the dangerous ones. And perhaps also less moral.[3]

Marsh, of course, acts on his philosophy, and in a showdown meeting with PECOCK in Rome tries to put the harness on him, at which point, in an outburst of rage, PECOCK bolts from the meeting site in disgust. It turns out that PECOCK's relationship with Rogers had been sanctioned by the political head of Fatah from the beginning. It was never a unilateral recruitment into a clandestine relationship, but it had worked because there had been a useful exchange of undertakings by both sides. The United States had not joined the Israeli effort to eliminate Fatah, and PECOCK had kept the United States informed of terrorist plots against Americans—a beneficial bargain. When Rogers is able to reestablish the relationship on that basis with PECOCK, the two collaborate until they are both killed, in separate bombing incidents.

Sometimes intelligence services attempt a more coercive approach. In Eric Ambler's *A Coffin for Dimitrios*, Karol Bulic, a Serbian employee of the Yugoslav Defense Ministry, is suborned by appealing to his self-conceit, greed, and zest for gambling. After the spymaster has established Bulic's access to Yugoslav plans to mine the Adriatic against incursions by the Italian fleet, Bulic is invited to a gambling den by an "international businessman" who implies a promise of future employment. Bulic is then lent some capital with which to gamble and maintain his pose as a worldly figure. He proceeds to lose badly, and the "businessman" pulls the string, forcing Bulic to steal the plans in order to satisfy his debt. The scheme eventually disintegrates into a farcical double cross by an operative named Dimitrios Makropoulos, but the point is established. In this espionage-for-hire caper, blackmail is the tool chosen to mount the recruitment. *A Coffin for Dimitrios* represents one of the better spy novels of the 1930s, after the epoch of the spy as protagonist and before the beginnings of World War II and Cold War spy fiction.

In real life, the British and American intelligence services have seldom banked on coercive recruitments because such recruitments contravene Anglo-Saxon legal and cultural norms and have been found, by and large, to produce unsatisfactory results. Whether that is because we are simply inept at blackmail, one can only conjecture. By contrast, the Soviet and Eastern European intelligence services have used women operatives to entrap Western businessmen and government officials in sexual liaisons in order to secure their cooperation in intelligence tasks. This technique, in spy vernacular a "honey trap," was particularly prevalent in Berlin and Vienna from 1946 on, but it was utilized most effectively in Moscow in the 1980s to ensnare U.S. Marine Corps Sergeant Clayton J. Lonetree. After he was confronted with photographs of his sexual dalliance with a female Soviet intelligence officer, Sergeant Lonetree was induced by the Soviet intelligence service to open the vaulted area of the U.S. embassy in Moscow to the Soviets for espionage purposes.

In addition to the traditional fee-for-service espionage recruitment, coerced or voluntary, there are some specialized versions. For example, Clarridge talks about "false flag" recruitments. While serving in India in 1963, he targeted a minor weekly newspaper which was espousing a strong pro-Chinese line in the ideological struggle between Soviet and Chinese Communism then taking place in southern India. He proposed to push the paper further and further to the left with the hope of prompting government intervention to suppress it. The publisher was Tamil, so to get in touch with him, Clarridge "borrowed" a support agent named Petros from outside India.

Petros didn't look Chinese, but on the other hand, he didn't look Indian either. "Eurasian" might fit. I brought him to Madras and gave him specific instructions: "Go see the pro-Chinese publisher. Tell him you have come from Beijing, or "the Center," as they call it. Offer him this stipend that he can't refuse, and recruit him on behalf of Beijing."

This would be a "false flag" recruitment—when an intelligence service recruits a target while pretending to represent another nation—a common piece of tradecraft. When you finally recruit the target, he believes he is providing information to some other nation. The Israelis have often used this technique by impersonating CIA officers when trying to recruit Arabs.[4]

In the event, the scheme worked brilliantly. The pro-Chinese publisher took the bait and was proud that his work had come to Beijing's attention. Again, the Soviets made abundant use of this technique during the Cold War. They succeeded in getting Soviet Bloc intelligence services to make recruitments on their behalf—West Germans were recruited by their East German brethren, for example. It permitted the sponsoring service to insulate itself from blowback if the recruitment attempt failed, and achieve greater success as well.

Some recruitment approaches stand very little chance of success but are mounted anyway, because the downside risk is dwarfed by the potential gain if the pitch is accepted. These are pitches where the case officer has had little or no opportunity to become acquainted with the target, to develop him to see if he might be amenable to such an approach. They are thus styled "cold pitches" or "gangplank" recruitment attempts.

Duane "Dewey" Clarridge
*CIA career operations officer
who supervised Aldrich Ames
on his first overseas tour in
Ankara, held increasingly
important positions in Near
Eastern and South Asian
matters in the Directorate of
Operations, and helped set up
the Counter-Terrorist Center
for the DCI. He was implicated
in the Iran-contra scandal
and eventually pardoned by
President George H. W. Bush.*

Clarridge describes a pitch to a Mongolian diplomat posted to India in 1961, who was about to be rotated home to Ulan Bator. The United States had no diplomatic relations with Mongolia at the time but was anxious to establish contacts with Mongolian officials, in order to prepare the way for formal ties. Clarridge made the pitch, without success, but confessed that although he had been called upon to make such cold approaches later, from a vantage point at the end of his career, he did not know of one that had succeeded.[5]

In the world of spy fiction, who can forget the attempt by George Smiley in India in 1955 to recruit his career nemesis, Karla, in John le Carré's *Tinker, Tailor, Soldier, Spy*? Karla was being summoned home to Moscow to face the music after the failure of an illegal's radio-connected espionage scheme in San Francisco. Smiley had a go at trying to get Karla to defect, from a stifling jail cell in Delhi, where the Indian intelligence service was holding him temporarily at the request of the British. Fruitlessly, he tried to appeal to Karla's humanity:

> "To sum it up, Karla was the proverbial cold-war orphan. He had left home to do a job abroad. The job had blown up in his face, but he couldn't go back: home was more hostile than abroad. We had no powers of permanent arrest, so it was up to Karla to ask us for protection. I don't think I had come across a clearer case for defection. I had only to convince him of the arrest of the San Francisco network—wave the press photographs and cuttings from my briefcase at him—talk to him a little about the unfriendly conspiracies of Brother Rudnev in Moscow, and cable the somewhat overworked inquisitors in Sarratt, and with any luck I'd make London by the weekend."[6]

Karla, of course, made no response to Smiley's offer, beyond walking off with Smiley's gold cigarette lighter and a pack of Camels. In answer to a question as to whether Karla had ever really thought of coming over:

> "I'm sure it never crossed his mind," said Smiley with disgust. "I behaved like a soft fool. The very archetype of a flabby Western liberal. But I would rather be my kind of fool than his, for all that. I am sure," he repeated vigorously, "that neither my arguments nor his own predicament at Moscow Centre would ultimately have swayed him in the least."[7]

Having established the traditional parameters of the recruitment game, do we find that recruitment pitches play out

GEORGE SMILEY
Le Carré's legendary spy catcher who was charged with finding the mole in the British Secret Intelligence Service in Tinker, Tailor, Soldier, Spy; portrayed here by Alec Guinness in the TV version.

according to these precepts? In the search for direction and control of a reporting agent, the understandings reached between recruiter and spy are as varied as human nature and the diverse cultures of the principal players. Dewey Clarridge pursued a Polish trade official posted in Istanbul for years before patience and a lucky opening permitted him to reel him in. By sheer persistence, Clarridge was able to get the ball rolling. He was able to persuade Mr. and Mrs. Adamski (ficti-tious names used in Clarridge's autobiography to protect the official and his wife because they are still alive) to come to din-ner at the Clarridge apartment and to maintain social contact for a time. Even in the West, and in a benign environment such as existed in Turkey in 1968, merely maintaining contact with a Soviet or Soviet Bloc official was a chore. An American official had to assume that if the Communist official continued to accept invitations, it probably meant that *he* was an intelligence officer deputed to try to recruit the American. Clarridge looked for indications that Adamski was simply what he appeared to be, a senior Polish trade official without an intelli-gence brief, and he found one when he encountered Adamski "unexpectedly" on a fishing expedition and Adamski clearly recognized him but concealed that fact from his embassy com-panions. Subsequently, Clarridge prevailed upon Adamski to meet with him alone over a bottle of scotch (the mother's milk of spy recruitments, but more on that later), only to discover that the Adamskis had completed their tour in Istanbul and were returning to Poland in several months' time. By this time, Clarridge was fairly certain that Adamski was what he appeared to be, a trade official, but it made no sense to pursue a recruit-ment attempt in May 1969 when the Adamskis were due to return home so soon. Years passed, and, as luck would have it, the Adamskis were assigned to Ankara in August 1971 at the same time as Clarridge became the CIA chief there. Despite several attempts, it took Clarridge more than a year to reestab-lish contact with his target, and in the event, the telephone call came from Adamski. He asked for an urgent meeting, and dur-ing the meeting he revealed to Clarridge that his wife, Irina, was pregnant. The significance of this revelation was not lost on Clarridge. If Irina was pregnant, the Adamskis would be required to return to Poland, which they emphatically did not want to do. Adamski asked Clarridge for help in obtaining an abortion. That was the hook. Over the objections of CIA head-quarters, Clarridge sought and obtained abortion pills from the Agency's regional medical officer and passed them to Adamski.

"In every operation there is an above the line and a below the line. Above the line is what you do by the book. Below the line is how you do the job."[8]

According to Adamski sometime later, Irina aborted natu-rally before she planned to take the pills, but Clarridge's rela-tionship with him was cemented by this willingness to help when he was in desperate need. Thereafter, Clarridge was able to get Adamski to accept intelligence requirements for secret information and to provide the information when he was able. The elaborate fan dance between the two had ended, and Adamski in effect was prepared to entrust Clarridge with his life and career.

In the subtlety of their civilization, the British appear to savor recruitment by indirection. *The Untouchable,* by John Banville,[9] is a loose depiction of the life of Anthony Blunt, the curator of the queen's portrait collection who was unmasked as one of the "Cambridge Five" spies for the Soviet Union in 1979. The novel contains a most remarkable description of Vic-tor Maskell's (Blunt's) recruitment by a central European fur trader named Felix Hartmann. Hartmann is styled on the Soviet illegal Teodor Maly, who helped recruit a number of the 1930s Cantabridgians. (Illegals are intelligence officers with assumed identities and no official connection to the employing power who recruit or handle spies. They operate out of embassy and have no diplomatic protection. The Soviets made great use of them during the 1930s and 1940s, a period often described in the former U.S.S.R. as the era of the "great illegals.")

After describing the philosophical and attitudinal furniture that cluttered the minds of these privileged products of Britain's class system, Banville has Hartmann begin by getting

Maskell to draft innocuous reports on European economic and political events. Then Hartmann pushes Maskell to join a targeted government department, and finally succeeds in getting him to bring out classified information, all in the guise of remaining true to his core beliefs: hatred of America ("The American occupation of Europe was to many of us not much less of a calamity than a German victory would have been"), fear of boredom, love of the double life ("Thus for us, everything was itself and at the same time something else"), and disdain for privilege at Cambridge, which at the height of the Depression contrasted vividly with the misery of the English masses and the sacrifice of the Republicans in the Spanish Civil War in 1936.[10] Banville describes how Maskell came to look at Marxism as "the faith of his fathers." "It is odd," Maskell noted, "how the small dishonesties are the ones that snag in the silk of the mind."[11]

Homosexuality, which was either a rite of passage or a lifetime commitment for many of the Cambridge aesthetes attracted to Communism at that time, played an unclear role in their recruitment. Both Blunt and Guy Burgess were homosexual and were active spotters for Soviet illegal recruiters Arnold Deutsch, Yuri Modin, and Teodor Maly. Whether a spy candidate's homosexuality was viewed as an element of vulnerability and thus a hook for recruitment, or whether it was merely a reflection of the mores of some in the social strata attracted to Communism at that time in Britain, remains a mystery.

It is remarkable that many of Banville's observations on the fictional Maskell's motivation for accepting recruitment by the Soviets for spying are substantiated in Miranda Carter's excellent new biography of Blunt.[12]

Are these elaborate recruitment schemes always necessary? The answer, thankfully for the spy runners, is that many spies recruit themselves. For a host of reasons, which I will explore, spies volunteer their services—for ideological reasons, for money, revenge, and power, and for love of the game of deception itself.

Dewey Clarridge, who served in the CIA for thirty years, holding increasingly responsible positions in the Directorate of Operations, and Robert M. Gates, who became director of central intelligence in the administration of the first President Bush, both acknowledged that they knew of no significant recruitments of Soviet spies during their long careers. The spies were all walk-ins, or volunteers. As Clarridge put it:

> Over time I came to believe that the Clandestine Services wasted a lot of emotional energy trying to recruit Soviets during the Cold War. Historically, those who really wanted to cooperate with the United States have walked in of their own volition and offered their services, usually for money. I know of no significant Soviet recruitment that was spotted, developed, and recruited from scratch by a CIA case officer. Likewise, those American traitors who went to work for the Soviets were invariably walk-ins.[13]

The term "walk-in" refers to the practice of a volunteer spy or defector literally walking into an embassy or official installation in a foreign country and offering his services to the officer or Marine on duty. This usually prompts a mad scramble to find out who the volunteer is; what he may know or be able to provide to the recipient government, especially if his information consists of warning of an imminent attack; and what the risks are of accepting his offer. In two of the most important Cold War cases involving Soviet volunteers, Popov and Penkovsky, these two Russian GRU officers literally had to throw themselves at Western officials before their offers to spy were taken up.

Pyotr Popov was a GRU (Soviet military intelligence) major who in 1953, in Vienna, dropped a letter offering to supply military information for money behind the front seat of an official car attached to the U.S. high commissioner for Austria. Popov was a Russian peasant with a grudge. He detested the Russian secret police in whatever form it had manifested itself, from the czar's Okhrana to the revolutionary Cheka to the KGB of 1952. He felt that the KGB represented the repressive arm of the Soviet state that had done nothing for the peasant backwater in which he had been raised, except make life there worse. His immediate need, however, was for money to pay for his Serbian girlfriend's abortion. In seeking out help from the West, he was willing to stay in place and provide whatever secret information he could get his hands on.

Oleg Penkovsky was a Soviet volunteer from the opposite end of the social spectrum. Also a GRU officer, Penkovsky had access through marriage and cleverly manipulated contacts to some of the most important technical military information in the Soviet state. But he too was deeply frustrated by the system. His father had been born to the near nobility and had in fact fought for the White Russian army in the 1920s, and Penkovsky believed that this fact kept him from rising further in his career, despite his own exemplary record in World War II and excellent performance thereafter as a GRU officer. After he made his decision to volunteer, he could not get anybody in the U.S., British, or Canadian embassy in Moscow to meet with him. He became so desperate that he approached two American tourists on the Moskvoretsky Bridge over the Moscow River on the rainy night of August 12, 1960, to ask them to deliver a packet of materials to a U.S. embassy official on his behalf.

Luckily, in both the Popov and Penkovsky cases the offers to spy, and the incriminating documents testifying to the men's access and identities, eventually found their way to officials able to act positively on them. Providentially, also, Soviet counterintelligence did not apprehend Popov and Penkovsky in their initial efforts to volunteer. It is clear evidence of Soviet success in intimidating Western governments with the thoroughness of their control over Soviet territory and Soviet citizens that, as volunteers, Popov and Penkovsky had to work so hard to convince their Western interlocutors of their bona fides and the fact that they were not KGB provocateurs.

Aldrich Ames encountered no similar difficulty when he walked into the Soviet embassy in Washington in April 1985 with what he valued at $150,000 worth of CIA and FBI secrets to sell to a Soviet intelligence officer, whose discretion and ability he already knew something about. Ames's motivation was primarily monetary. He believed he had big bills to pay: alimony for his first wife and support for a woman with extravagant tastes who was soon to become his second wife. As we shall see, however, this was not the entire story.

What makes people agree to spy? What causes them to turn their backs on home and family and agree to betray their trust? What is the motivation?

Let's begin with ideology. If one may generalize, the Cambridge Five became so disgusted with the privilege that surrounded them at Cambridge University, in contrast to the economic calamity that had engulfed the lives of so many ordinary Britons in the midst of the Great Depression, that they were open to the blandishments of Arnold Deutsch, a brilliant Soviet illegal and scholar who befriended them at university. Deutsch was a Hungarian Jew who had received his Ph.D. in Vienna at the age of twenty-four, and who used his considerable charm and intellect to convince these sensitive and impressionable young gentlemen that the Soviet Union was creating a progressive worker-peasant paradise in Russia that represented a more humane alternative to the destructive force of American-style market capitalism which had laid Europe low. When the

U.S.S.R. proved to be the only European nation willing to oppose Francisco Franco's campaign to drive the Republican government from power in Spain in 1936, and with the horror of Hitler's nascent war machine taking battle practice at Franco's side, several of the Cambridge elite followed their classmate John Cornford into the struggle in which he lost his life. A comparable reaction was doubtless elicited in similar intellectual circles in the United States. It took news of the extent of Stalin's purges of Soviet citizens from 1938 on, and the conclusion of the Stalin-Ribbentrop Pact in 1939, to convince all but the most die-hard Communists that Stalin's paradise was a chimera. Nonetheless, Philby, Blunt, Burgess, Donald Maclean, and John Cairncross soldiered on in Britain in the service of the Soviet state, as did Julius and Ethel Rosenberg, Harry Dexter White, and Alger Hiss in the United States.

By the early 1950s, the appeal of Soviet Communism as a basis for ideological recruitment of spies in the West had all but disappeared. It was in this period that the British and U.S. intelligence services began to score some recruitment successes of their own against the Soviets on an ideological basis. During the effort at thawing out from the Cold War after the death of Stalin in 1953, Nikita Khrushchev was under pressure to liberalize the domestic economy. It soon became manifest that he would not be able to do so under the stultifying weight of central planning and control, and still meet the Soviet Presidium's foreign policy and defense goals. As a consequence, volunteers like Popov and Penkovsky offered their services to the West for a variety of reasons, not the least of which was disillusionment with Khrushchev and the Soviet system.

However, the decision of a spy to commit treason by supplying secret information to a foreign power is a complex one made up of a savory stew of emotions. Popov needed money, but he also hated the security apparatus of the Soviet state and Stalin's willful neglect of Russia's poor rural peasantry.

Penkovsky was frustrated by his inability to advance in rank in the Soviet system, but he also had greatly admired the U.S. army attaché in Ankara in 1955–1956, Colonel Charles Maclean Peeke, with whom he had served, and he wanted to help the United States and Britain understand Khrushchev's irrational saber-rattling, which might otherwise lead to nuclear war.

On the U.S. side, Aldrich Ames needed money, but he also was frustrated that his career had stalled at the journeyman level of GS-14. (That was the salary level of his job under the federal government's General Schedule, which the CIA followed, although it was not required to do so. At the time of Ames's betrayal, GS-14 paid about $65,000 per year.) Ames believed that colleagues who were less able than he had been promoted ahead of him. The evidence also suggests that by the early 1980s, Ames had lost the professional faith of CIA officers that the Soviet Union represented a mortal threat to the United States. Whether as rationalization for his treachery or from genuine belief, Ames began to view the declining U.S.S.R. as more the victim of the West's continuing Cold War psychosis than a genuine enemy. As a consequence, he viewed the spy wars between the United States and U.S.S.R. as episodes in a long-running sporting contest in which each side knew the risks and rewards of the game. If he ratted on a Soviet spying for the West, he would be eliminating either a player whom the Soviets already knew about and were running as a double agent, or one who had assumed the risk in his espionage that he might one day be betrayed. In Ames's view, there was no reason to get upset over such a development. It was just the way the game was played.

The motivation to accept recruitment to commit espionage is equally mixed in spy literature. In Graham Greene's *The Human Factor,* the protagonist, Maurice Castle, is told by the visiting chief of South African intelligence that the South

African Communist who had saved Castle's agent (and soon-to-be wife) and her young son had died in prison:

> "I used to tell him he wasn't a real Communist."
>
> "Why? He was a member of the Party. One of the oldest members left in the Transvaal."
>
> "Of course. I know that. But there are members and members, aren't there? . . ."
>
> "He had a way of drawing people to him."
>
> "Most of the Communists I knew—they pushed, they didn't draw."
>
> "All the same, Sarah, he was a genuine Communist. He survived Stalin like Roman Catholics survived the Borgias. He made me think better of the Party."
>
> "But he never drew you that far, did he?"
>
> "Oh, there were always some things which stuck in my throat. He used to say I strained at a gnat and swallowed a camel. You know I was never a religious man—I left God behind in the school chapel, but there were priests I sometimes met in Africa who made me believe again—for a moment—over a drink. If all priests had been like they were and I had seen them often enough, perhaps I would have swallowed the Resurrection, the Virgin birth, Lazarus, the whole works. . . . For a while I half believed in his God, like I half believed in Carson's. Perhaps I was born to be a half-believer. When people talk about Prague and Budapest and how you can't find a human face in Communism I stay silent. Because I've seen—once—the human face. I say to myself that if it hadn't been for Carson, Sam would have been born in a prison and you would probably have died in one. One kind of Communism—or

Communist—saved you and Sam. I don't have any trust in Marx or Lenin any more than I have in Saint Paul, but haven't I the right to be grateful?"

"Why do you worry so much about it? No one would say you were wrong to be grateful, I'm grateful too. Gratitude's all right if . . ."

"If . . . ?"

"I think I was going to say if it doesn't take you too far."[14]

But, of course, it had taken him too far. In his fit of gratitude, Castle had betrayed his section in MI6, unwittingly helped the Soviets protect a double agent in the British service, and compromised a major British–American–South African scheme called Uncle Remus that was designed to preserve apartheid.

Two

Betrayal

"Betrayal," she said. " 'We betray to be loyal.
Betrayal is like imagining when the reality isn't good
enough.' He wrote that. Betrayal as hope and compensation. As the making of a better land. Betrayal
as love. As a tribute to our unlived lives. On and on,
these ponderous aphorisms about betrayal. Betrayal
as escape. As a constructive act. As a statement of
ideals. Worship. As an adventure of the soul. . . ."[1]

These lines uttered by Mary Pym as she pores over the writings
of her fugitive husband, Magnus, in le Carré's *A Perfect Spy*
illustrate a view of betrayal that appears to turn the normal
moral order on its head. Yet they are not so distant from the tone
of the observations admitted FBI spy Robert P. Hanssen wrote
to his Russian intelligence handlers during his period of service
to the Russians after 1985. The communications contained in
the affidavit filed by the U.S. government at the time of
Hanssen's indictment in February 2001 indicate a twisted
approach to the work he was doing for the Russians, in which
Hanssen appeared to take a perverse pride in using his inside
position and knowledge to benefit a rival and potentially hostile
power. He claimed that he had always wanted to be a spy since
reading Kim Philby's autobiography at the age of fourteen

(although he was wrong about the timing, since Philby's autobiography was published in 1968 and Hanssen would have been twenty-four); the implication is that he derived great professional satisfaction from deceiving his FBI colleagues.

A similar intoxication by deception appears to have motivated Anthony Blunt as well.[2]

Betrayal, of course, is what distinguishes espionage from most other human transgressions. To provide secret information to a foreign country is a treasonous act. It is not like stealing a loaf of bread. And once the spy has performed an act of espionage there is no possibility of return. The Rubicon has been crossed. The betrayal of trust is permanent and irredeemable. Once violated, trust can never be restored.

Which is why Aldrich Ames followed his sale of $150,000 worth of "unimportant" spies to the Soviets in April 1985 with "the big dump" in June of that year, in which he gave away every spy case the United States was running against the Soviets at the time, and every intelligence operation against the U.S.S.R. of which he was aware. He claimed he had done it to protect his own neck. If one of the spies he betrayed in June had become aware from his April offering that he was a mole in the CIA, that fact might have been reported to U.S. intelligence in due course. The easiest way to deal with that risk was to eliminate it, Ames believed. In fact, once he started down the road of espionage and betrayal, there was no turning back, and in his view, he might as well exploit his insider position to the hilt.

We do not yet know the precise details (and we may never know them), but Robert P. Hanssen appears to have confessed his spying to a Catholic priest in 1991, after having been caught in the act by his spouse. He is said to have promised to stop spying and to give his ill-gotten gains to charity, but his redemption appears to have been short-lived. He was back at it by the end of the decade.

The point is that betrayal will eat at the soul of a spy unless he has forged a suit of armor against it. If the spy's motivation is ideological or monetary, or it springs from revenge or a lust for power, that may mitigate the corrosive effects of betraying one's trust, but for most ordinary mortals, it is difficult to lead a double life for an extended period of time. It is hard to remember all the lies that need to be told to pull it off.

And it plays hell with the life of the spy runner who has to deal with the idiosyncrasies betrayal produces, as CIA case officer George Kisevalter, who ran both Popov and Penkovsky, could attest. Some, like Popov, became cavalier about their own personal security and took risks that endangered the operation. They must have understood that intellectually, but they took the risks anyway. Popov brought a huge permanent exhibit showing the Soviet Order of Battle out of GRU Headquarters at the Imperial Hotel in Vienna in 1951; if the exhibit had been missed during its short absence or spotted under his military tunic, Popov would certainly have been arrested. Likewise, Penkovsky insisted upon making regular brush passes in Moscow with the wife of a British diplomat who was his regular contact long after it was regarded as safe to do so by his handlers.

Aldrich Ames removed book bags of classified operational espionage traffic, some of it original cables, from CIA Headquarters in Langley to give to his Soviet case officer in Washington. If he had been stopped randomly by a security guard or observed in the taking by one of his colleagues, this operation would not have run for nine years.

Were these breaches of rudimentary operational security mere lapses on the part of the experienced spies who committed them, or were they indicators of a different sort, suggesting that in their betrayal, the spies were clamoring for a kind of recognition that only great risk taking would satisfy? In reading Jerrold Schecter and Peter Deriabin's excellent study of Penkovsky entitled *The Spy Who Saved the World*, one must

ALDRICH AMES

The CIA's most damaging mole or spy during the Cold War. His betrayal to the Soviets in 1985 caused the deaths of at least ten Soviet agents spying for the United States at the time and compromised a great number of operations and people working against the Soviet Union until his arrest in 1994.

take note of the observations of a CIA psychiatrist who had studied defectors and determined that a common characteristic is self-identification as a "wronged person who elevates his private dissatisfaction into a political principle."[3] The CIA psychiatrist, Alan Studner, also identified a strain of narcissism which is more than self-love. It is pathologic self-absorption, a preoccupation with the self at the expense of others. Dr. Studner claimed that Penkovsky believed himself abused by a system that did not credit his superior abilities and therefore had lost its claim to his loyalty. He believed he possessed leadership qualities and was a mover of history—attributes that should have led to his promotion to field rank but were unrecognized. Finally, he was supremely overconfident. "He could not imagine he would get caught. Normal mortals get caught, not a child of destiny with a vision," Dr. Studner explained.[4]

These observations might well have been made on a less grandiose scale about Aldrich Ames. They are probably less descriptive of Popov, who in the end never divested himself of his genuine persona as a Russian peasant, hard-drinking, as loyal to his mistress as to his family and his origins, and highly disapproving of Stalin's repressive Soviet state. He needed money, to be sure, but he was very happily willing to betray a system in which he had no stake and for which he had no sympathy.

In the real world of espionage, however, Kim Philby was the ultimate betrayer of the Cold War era. Born to privilege, the son of a noted scholar and Arabist, Harold "Kim" Philby was "one of us," like Conrad's Lord Jim. It was inconceivable to his contemporaries in British and U.S. intelligence that Philby could have been an ideological Communist, much less a spy for the Soviet Union. He bamboozled not only the leading lights of the British intelligence service but also his high-ranking contacts in the CIA such as Frank Wisner and James J. Angleton, and he did untold damage to British and American efforts to roll back the Iron Curtain in the years after World War II.

His autobiography, *My Silent War*, written long after his defection, is itself a masterpiece of gray propaganda, giving no hint of emotional turmoil at the deception he had lived and the damage his betrayal had caused. He notes simply:

> All through my career, I have been a straight penetration agent working in the Soviet interest. The fact that I joined the British Secret Intelligence Service is neither here nor there; I regarded my SIS appointments purely in the light of cover-jobs, to be carried out sufficiently well to ensure my attaining positions in which my service to the Soviet Union

would be most effective. My connection with SIS must be seen against my prior total commitment to the Soviet Union which I regarded then, as I do now, as the inner fortress of the world movement.[5]

The only hint Philby gives of his motivation is reminiscent of the utterance of Maurice Castle, in the extract from Graham Greene's *The Human Factor* included in the previous chapter, expressing his gratitude at having seen the human face of Communism. After describing the trial to his faith posed by his knowledge that "much was going badly wrong in the Soviet Union,"[6] Philby quotes approvingly from another Graham Greene work, *The Confidential Agent,* in which the heroine asks the hero if his leaders are any better than the others.

"No. Of course not," he replies. "But I still prefer the people they lead—even if they lead them all wrong."
"The poor, right or wrong," she scoffed. "It's no worse—is it?—than my country, right or wrong. You choose your side once and for all—of course, it may be the wrong side. Only history can tell that."[7]

Philby chose his side, seemingly without a trace of remorse with regard to the institutions and the friendships this would cause him to betray. And he stuck with his choice even after his defection in the early 1950s caused him to finish his life in a dreary Moscow apartment without particular notice or reward.

Le Carré models Bill Haydon in *Tinker, Tailor, Soldier, Spy* after Philby. Haydon is as unmarked by the treachery he has been part of as Philby declared himself to be:

Haydon had betrayed. As a lover, a colleague, a friend; as a patriot; as a member of that inestimable body that Ann loosely called the Set: in every capacity, Haydon had overtly pursued one aim and secretly achieved its opposite. Smiley knew very well that even now he did not grasp the scope of that appalling duplicity; yet there was a part of him that rose already in Haydon's defence. Was not Bill also betrayed? Connie's lament rang in his ears: "Poor loves. Trained to Empire, trained to rule the waves . . . You're the last, George, you and Bill." He saw with painful clarity an ambitious man born to the big canvas, brought up to rule, divide and conquer, whose visions and vanities all were fixed, like Percy's, upon the world's game; for whom the reality was a poor island with scarcely a voice that would carry across the water. . . .[8]

It is apparent that part of what was going on with Philby and Haydon was their resistance to the passing of the mantle of leadership from Britain to "the cousins" in North America. Nonetheless, as le Carré makes clear from his examination of the human detritus created by Haydon/Philby's betrayal, there is no abstract idea of a greater public good that can justify these traitorous acts. Haydon's punishment is swift and final.

Despite the enormity of the rupture represented by a spy's decision to abandon his family, friends, and colleagues and betray his trust, most real spies appear to have been largely untroubled by the consequences. Perhaps the greed, thirst for revenge, lust for power, or search for vindication underlying the spy's decision to betray overpowers all other emotions, but there is evidence that as time passes, some spies are affected by the hole they have dug for themselves.

The U.S. government affidavits in the Robert Hanssen case suggest that before his arrest, Hanssen had premonitions that the "sleeping dogs were awakening" and the authorities were closing in on him. There is a further intimation that an end to his double life might not have been unwelcome.

Popov continually took unnecessary operational risks in contacting his case officer, handing a letter with contact instructions to an unknown pair of British military attachés in East Germany, for example, and ignoring his emergency contact plan, after he had long been out of touch with his American handler in Germany. Penkovsky pushed personal meetings with his British intelligence handler, Greville Wynne, past the number that could be justified by Wynne's overt position as a private businessman. Finally, Aldrich Ames made no effort to conceal the enormous amounts of money he spent on monthly credit card payments, automobiles, clothes, and the purchase of his principal residence in Arlington, Virginia, for $540,000 in cash, which could not be justified by his modest government salary.

In each case, one might argue that the spy's disregard for his own security was a product of overconfidence, his belief that he was a master of his espionage universe and that nobody in the exploited institutions was clever enough to catch him. An equally cogent argument can be made that over time the strains of maintaining the deception of a double life impacted on each of these spies so that each behaved as if he did not care if he was found out.

John le Carré's fictional obsession with the burden of betrayal in *A Perfect Spy* may emanate from roots more personal than the verisimilitude of his ordinary observations on the world of espionage. Critics have speculated that Rick Pym, the protagonist's father, is modeled on the author's father, who in his son's recollection was a notorious confidence man:

> "So will I," Pym promised loyally and meant every word. Like Rick he was learning to live on several planes at once. The art of it was to forget everything

except the ground you stood on and the face you spoke from at that moment."[9]

Having observed a lifetime of his father's betrayals and having an affinity for betrayal himself, Magnus Pym is finally liberated by his father's death:

Rick should have died when I killed him. Pym whispered the words out loud, daring himself to hear it. "You should have died when I killed you." . . . Love is whatever you can still betray, he thought. Betrayal can only happen if you love.[10]

Whether or not *A Perfect Spy* is partly autobiographical, le Carré's obsession with betrayal makes for a brilliant piece of spy fiction. Although it is perhaps slightly overdrawn as a reflection of the spy's real dilemma, its denouement is riveting and fun:

"Sir Magnus, you have in the past betrayed me but, more important, you have betrayed yourself. Even when you are telling the truth, you lie. You have loyalty and you have affection. But to what? To whom? I don't know all the reasons for this. Your great father. Your aristocratic mother. One day maybe you will tell me. And maybe you have put your love in some bad places now and then." He leaned forward and there was a kindly, true affection in his face and a warm long-suffering smile in his eyes. "Yet you also have morality. You search. What I am saying is, Sir Magnus: for once nature has produced a perfect match. You are a perfect spy. All you need is a cause. I have it. I know that our revolution is young and that sometimes the wrong people are running it. In the pursuit of peace we are making too much war. In the pursuit of freedom we are building too many prisons. But in the long run I don't mind. Because I know this. All the junk that made you what you are: the privileges, the snobbery, the hypocrisy, the churches, the schools, the fathers, the class systems, the historical lies, the little lords of the countryside, the little lords of big business, and all the greedy wars that result from them, we are sweeping that away for ever. For your sake. Because we are making a society that will never produce such sad fellows as Sir Magnus." He held out his hand. "So I've said it. You are a good man and I love you."[11]

To show that this appeal to a con man/spy is just as transparently disingenuous as all the earlier scams that the speaker, Axel, has lived through with Magnus, including Magnus's earlier betrayal of him to his British intelligence boss, Jack Brotherhood, and the Swiss police, le Carré concludes: "And I remember that touch always. I can see it any time by looking into my own palm: dry and decent and forgiving. And the laughter: from the heart as it always was, once he had ceased to be *tactical* [italics added] and become my friend again."[12]

As Graham Greene observed in his epigraph to *The Human Factor*, quoting from Joseph Conrad: "I only know that he who forms a tie is lost. The germ of corruption has entered into his soul."[13] Magnus Pym's ties were too many, and the corruption was total.

Three

The Spy Bureaucracy

"There's just one thing I think you ought to know before you take on this job. And don't forget it. If you do well you'll get no thanks and if you get into trouble you'll get no help. Does that suit you?" . . .

He shook hands with Ashenden and showed him out. Ashenden was well aware that he would never know what happened then. Being no more than a tiny rivet in a vast and complicated machine, he never had the advantage of seeing a completed action. He was concerned with the beginning or the end of it, perhaps, or with some incident in the middle, but what his own doings led to he had seldom a chance of discovering. It was as unsatisfactory as those modern novels that give you a number of unrelated episodes and expect you by piecing them together to construct in your mind a connected narrative.[1]

These passages from W. Somerset Maugham's *Ashenden* herald the entry of a new player on the scene, the spy bureaucracy which employs and directs the spies and spy runners who collect secret information from foreign countries by illegal means. Although their existence dates from the beginning in the real world, official organizations dedicated to espionage appear relatively recently as subjects of comment in spy literature. *Ashenden,* incidentally, was first published in 1927 and served as a sort of training aid or trot for the British intelligence services in the 1930s.

In Kipling's *Kim,* there are references to Colonel Creighton and Sahib Lurgan, whose decisions impact directly on Kim's education and training in preparation for a role in the Great Game, but there is a minimum of paperwork and structure governing his espionage activities in India. Hurree Babu, Kim's Bengali superior, promises Kim honorable mention in his account of the caper by which Kim has separated the papers and maps from a traveling Frenchman and Russian to further the interests of the Raj, but there is little more organizational presence than that in the book.

In *The Riddle of the Sands,* by Erskine Childers, and *The Thirty-nine Steps,* by John Buchan, the protagonists are the spies. They are volunteers, not responding to direction from any institutional source. However, Davies and Carruthers in *Riddle* and Richard Hannay in *The Thirty-nine Steps* recognize that the intelligence they have collected will be of great interest to their government spy organizations when they finally make contact and report in.

It is only when one gets to World War II and the Cold War that the spy bureaucracies become a factor in fictional accounts of espionage. Because the world was seeing in the actions of Hitler and Stalin that these two totalitarians were capable of completely controlling the lives of the citizens in their police states in ways that departed radically from their historical moral and cultural values, and were exhibiting a strong determination to extend the reach of both fascist and Communist power to their neighbors, the West was shocked into a reaction. World War II represented the Allied nations' reaction to Axis fascist aggression; the Marshall Plan, NATO, and the Cold War policies of containment and rollback represented the response to Stalin's Communist expansionism. The U.S. created the Central Intelligence Agency at the same time that the British strengthened their intelligence services to deal with Communist subversion. During the ten years following its creation in 1947, the CIA was assigned the task of countering the spread of Communism using Stalin's own methods: propaganda, payments to Western political parties, sabotage, funding guerrilla movements, and engaging in all-out spy wars. Leading American statesmen penned official government directives, for example, National Security Council Directive 68, signed by President Truman, calling on the United States to use the same techniques against the spread of Soviet totalitarianism that the Soviets were using against the West. Fight fire with fire, the CIA was being urged.

It is in the 1950s that one begins to encounter in the literature the implied question of whether, in treating the Soviets with their own medicine, the West was not abandoning the high ground and descending into the moral gutter of deceit, betrayal, and manipulation. If it was, what then separated our human values from theirs?

Alec Leamas expresses this viewpoint with passion in le Carré's *The Spy Who Came In from the Cold*,[2] published in 1963. After losing his top East German agent in a shoot-out at a West Berlin crossing point, weather-beaten MI6 operative Alec Leamas is brought back to London, "in from the cold," only to become the central figure in a byzantine scheme hatched by Control, SIS chief of service, to save Britain's most productive East German spy. The spy Control is trying to save, Hans-Dieter Mundt, however, is a detestable figure, a former Hitler youth, who was recruited while serving in the United Kingdom as the head of the East German Steel mission. Recently, Mundt, who has risen to head East German intelligence, has come under suspicion by his own deputy, Fiedler, who has been tracking Mundt's movements in Europe and correlating them with suspicious deposits into Mundt's bank account. Fiedler is Mundt's direct opposite: a Jew and convinced Communist who is fiercely loyal to the East German worker state. Control's scheme is to have Leamas pretend to go to seed and, after coming to the attention of the East German spy network, defect and reveal to Fiedler information that would corroborate Mundt's guilt. Unbeknown to Leamas, Control plans to turn the tables on Fiedler through the instrumentality of Leamas's Elizabeth Bentley–type sweetheart, an idealistic British Communist named Liz Gold. Liz is called to testify at Mundt's trial, and she reveals to the court, by indirection, top SIS involvement in the scheme that Leamas believed he was furthering: namely, planting the seed that Mundt is probably a British spy. Mundt is freed, Fiedler is incarcerated, and Mundt arranges for Leamas and Liz to escape at night over the Berlin Wall. There is one final double cross when Liz is shot as she tries to climb the Wall, and in his disgust at being manipulated by his own side, Leamas allows himself to be gunned down too.

What has ensured Leamas's place in the pantheon of Cold War spy fiction greats is his answers to the questions Liz poses as they make their escape. She recounts the facts as she sees them: the cruel manipulation of her sympathy and innocent love for Leamas by British intelligence; the evil Mundt represents, even if he is London's agent; and the more admirable character of Fiedler. After screaming that she and Alec have been used and cheated by impersonal, uncaring big-power forces, and that the wrong man has been saved, she demands that Leamas answer: Which side is he on? Good or evil?

Leamas blurts out in response:

> "There's only one law in this game. . . . Mundt is
> their man; he gives them what they need. That's easy
> enough to understand, isn't it? Leninism—the expe-

diency of temporary alliances. What do you think spies are: priests, saints and martyrs? They're a squalid procession of vain fools, traitors too, yes; pansies, sadists and drunkards, people who play cowboys and Indians to brighten their rotten lives. Do you think they sit like monks in London, balancing the rights and wrongs? I'd have killed Mundt if I could, I hate his guts; but not now. It so happens that they need him. They need him so that the great moronic mass you admire can sleep soundly in their beds at night. They need him for the safety of ordinary, crummy people like you and me."[3]

In the real world, the known instances of organizational behavior by spy bureaucracies that are most closely comparable to Control's starkly amoral exploitation of Leamas reveal more about bureaucratic ineptitude than cold calculation. In the Bay of Pigs fiasco of April 1961, the decision by top management to exclude the analytical side of the CIA from involvement in planning the covert invasion of Cuba owed more to a misplaced notion of "need to know" principles than to malignant design. If the Agency's analysts had been consulted in early 1961 as to whether a ragtag group of fifteen hundred inadequately trained guerrillas had any chance of succeeding in landing on a remote and inhospitable Cuban shore, against an increasingly confident pro-Castro defense force, they would have replied in unanimity, "Hell, no!" Indeed, as Christopher Andrew notes in For the President's Eyes Only, former Marine officer, Harvard law professor, and then deputy director of intelligence Bob Amory, who was excluded by Director of Central Intelligence Allen Dulles from official knowledge of the pending Bay of Pigs invasion, exclaimed upon learning details of the operation that he had made more amphibious landings in the South Pacific in World War II as a soldier than the

ALEC LEAMAS

The celebrated protagonist of le Carré's The Spy Who Came In
from the Cold *who first pitched the argument that Western spy
services had lost their moral compass and were capable of acting as
ruthlessly as the Soviet spy services in pursuit of quasi-moral goals;
portrayed here by Richard Burton in the film version.*

Marine colonel planning the invasion, and he did not think
much of the plans.[4]

There were a number of additional things that went wrong
with the Bay of Pigs: President John F. Kennedy's inexperience
with covert operations and lack of enthusiasm for this one; the
absurd adherence to the doctrine of "plausible deniability" that

kept the U.S. military from playing a more central role in the operation and, more important, perhaps salvaging it; and the lack of operational security, with Miami Cubans and their families blabbing to the press about the forthcoming invasion in the months before it took place.

The Leamas-like problem it presents, however, is slightly different. When Jake Esterline and Colonel Jack Hawkins came to Richard Bissell in early 1961, threatening to resign in protest over President Kennedy's decision to relocate the site of the invasion to the Bay of Pigs to make the operation "quieter," Bissell talked them into staying the course, by implying that JFK would not let the operation fail once he gave it the green light. What he apparently said in addition was more troublesome. He left the impression with Esterline and Hawkins that having convened the guerrilla band, and having trained them to believe that they would soon be turned loose on the island, the United States would have a major disposal problem consisting of disgruntled Cubans if the operation did not go forward as planned. How would the United States be able to tell them to return to their homes—that the time was no longer ripe for a guerrilla onslaught? And how could their obvious disgust and disillusionment be contained?

Bissell was the deputy director for operations at the CIA and as such was in direct command of the Bay of Pigs operation. He was a brilliant former economics professor who had come to Washington during World War II, and who had held a high-ranking position dispensing Marshall Plan aid after the war. Allen Dulles brought him to the CIA in the 1950s and put him in charge of realizing the U-2 project, which Bissell did, working with Kelly Johnson at Lockheed's "skunk works." He had had next to no experience with human spies. During the more than yearlong training of the guerrillas in Florida and Central America, Bissell never visited the training camps to take the measure of the invasion force he was about to unleash.

If part of his decision process was to go forward with the invasion in the circumstances of April 1961, which were vastly altered from those that had existed at the beginning of planning for it a year earlier, because the U.S. could not say no to the guerrillas, this would have been a perfect illustration of the covert action tail wagging the operational dog in Cold War espionage. It would not have exhibited the malice aforethought of Control's manipulation of Leamas.

The decision to proceed may also have reflected Bissell's hope and expectation that Fidel Castro would fall victim to one of the Agency's many abortive assassination attempts before the event, thus obviating the need for an invasion. In any case, Robert F. Kennedy's instant determination to find a way to rescue the prisoners taken by Castro's forces on the beaches of the Bay of Pigs further argues for the proposition that the Kennedy administration had not washed its hands of responsibility for the failed invasion.

A second fictional assault on the mores that govern a spy organization's loyalty to its agents is set forth in Ignatius's *Agents of Innocence.* Tom Rogers's agent PECOCK is believed by the Israelis to be behind the Black September attack on the Israeli Olympic team in Munich in September 1972. Somehow the Israelis discover that CIA is running PECOCK as an agent. They ask the Director of Central Intelligence as head of an allied service to turn him over. The Director is about to accede, and proposes to do so to his top Middle East deputy, Edward Stone; Tom Rogers, PECOCK's case officer; and the chief of Beirut station, Frank Hoffman, in the course of an official visit. This provokes the following exchange with Hoffman:

> "The Israelis have asked for our help in dealing with Black September. They have implied, but not said directly, that they would like us to do one of two things: either provide them with some of the intelli-

gence we're getting from Ramlawi [PECOCK], or help them find him."

"And suppose we tell them to fuck off?" said Hoffman.

"They have made it clear that they intend to kill the leaders of Black September, including Ramlawi."

"What did you tell them, Director, if you don't mind my asking?"

"I told them we would get back to them."

"I trust, sir, that you didn't in any way confirm their speculation that we have been in contact with Ramlawi?"

"Of course not," said the Director. "That would be unprofessional."

"You're God-damned right it would be, sir," said Hoffman.

The Director narrowed his eyes. He was a man who prided himself on his composure. He displayed emotion rarely, and only when he was very angry.

"Easy, Frank," said Stone gently.

"I apologize, Director. But this whole conversation makes me very uneasy, to be honest."

"And why is that?" asked the Director.

"Because what the Israelis are proposing is totally outrageous. We should be telling them to take a walk, instead of driving ourselves crazy like this. Ramlawi may be the biggest shit who ever lived. But he met with us in good faith. We shouldn't throw him to the wolves now, just because it may be expedient. When we decide to work with someone, we make an implicit promise that we're not going to shop him to the next guy that comes along."

"Oh come now," said the Director. "Let's grow up.

We shop people every day. That's part of our business."

That remark seemed to touch an especially raw nerve in Hoffman. He grew red in the face.

"I don't need any lectures about the real world, Director. I may not have gone to Yale, it's true. But that doesn't mean I don't understand the way the world works. I've been running agents for nearly thirty years. In that time, I have screwed enough people simply because someone from Yale told me to. I don't want to do it again."

"Don't press your luck, Mr. Hoffman," said the Director.

Hoffman ignored the warning.

"We used to have a saying in the FBI," he said. "It was very simple: 'Protect your sources.' Even the dumbest FBI agent understands that. He knows that when someone trusts you, you don't knife him in the back. But I guess we're too smart for that in the agency."[5]

The argument intensifies, until Stone makes it clear that he, Rogers, and Hoffman will all three resign if the Director shops PECOCK to the Israelis. They arrive at a compromise in which it is agreed that CIA will not help the Israelis get PECOCK, but it won't help PECOCK stay alive either. It will remain neutral. The upshot is that Hoffman retires in disgust, PECOCK is killed by a "terrorist" bomb, probably planted by the Israelis, and Rogers is killed in the Beirut embassy bombing. The Middle East lumbers along in its continual cycle of ethnic hatred and violence.

Ignatius puts the matter in perspective with the observations of the station's oldest recruited spy, who reflects on the role of the Agency in the Arab world in a letter to Hoffman:

"The agency was the part of America that I liked the best, the part that understood the way the world is. It is easy to have the ideals of a twenty-year-old, but you need the cunning of a fifty-year-old to achieve them. When I met you and Mr. Rogers, I thought, Maybe there is a chance. Maybe these Americans have the toughness. I thought: These men are cynical enough to do good. And that was when I began to think that America truly could liberate the Arab world.

"I was wrong. Americans are not hard men. Even the CIA has a soft heart. You want so much to achieve good and make the world better, but you do not have the stomach for it. And you do not know your limitations. You are innocence itself. You are the agents of innocence. That is why you make so much mischief. You come into a place like Lebanon as if you were missionaries. You convince people to put aside their old customs and allegiances and to break the bonds that hold the country together. With your money and your schools and your cigarettes and music, you convince us that we can be like you. But we can't. And when the real trouble begins, you are gone. And you leave your friends, the ones who trusted you most, to die.

"I will tell you what it is. You urge us to open up the windows of heaven. But you do not realize that the downpour will come rushing through and drown us all."[6]

Ignatius has here expressed a sentiment about the role of American power in the Middle East identical to that which Graham Greene articulated about the United States in Asia in *The Quiet American,* but with less wormwood and gall.

The reality, as you might suppose, is slightly different. When the Clinton administration, prodded by Congress, decided to try covert action in 1994 to unseat Saddam Hussein after Operation Desert Storm by sponsoring a revolt in the north of Iraq among the Kurdish population, the revolt ended unsuccessfully in fratricidal struggle between two Kurdish factions, one controlled by an Iranian element and the other by an Iraqi. It became necessary to evacuate the leaders of the anti-Saddam faction, whom the U.S. was directing and paying, on an emergency basis. But evacuate where? These operatives, intelligence officers, saboteurs, guerrilla warriors, and thugs were as unwelcome in both Iran and Iraq as quarrelsome Kurds have been in that part of the world for centuries. The United States agreed to move them to a U.S. possession, Guam, but only as a temporary effort at resettlement. It was clear that the U.S. Immigration and Naturalization Service (INS) would not admit these "freedom fighters" to the United States any more enthusiastically than it did the Meo tribesmen who fought for the CIA in Laos in the late 1960s or the mujahedeen who helped chase the Soviets out of Afghanistan in the 1980s. Some of the Saddam oppositionists allegedly had criminal records or were thought to be pro-Saddam Iraqi intelligence officers. Although the details of this operation have never been investigated or publicized (except in Robert Baer's *See No Evil*),[7] Iraqi refugees were eventually required to depart Guam and were incarcerated near Los Angeles pending the outcome of a secret INS administrative hearing called to determine their fate. The situation was Kafkaesque.

At this point, former director of central intelligence James Woolsey appeared in the case for the Iraqi spies on a pro bono basis and asked to see the classified information that was being argued by the U.S. government as the basis for refusing to admit them as immigrants. After an initial refusal, Woolsey was permitted to see some of the accusations against those agents whom the United States had been prepared to send against Saddam but was unwilling to admit to U.S. shores after the operation collapsed. He was outraged. Much of the so-called evidence was apparently unsupported, one-sided statements of unidentified informants, and Woolsey blew the case out of the water. The irony was that the CIA, under a provision of law dating from 1949, had the right to admit one hundred aliens each year, no questions asked, but apparently refused to even consider using it in this case. This is not how a reputation is forged in the spy business for looking after your own.

Some years earlier, Dewey Clarridge had summed up the attitude of a number of experienced case officers of his generation to the perceived tendency of the spy bureaucracy to leave its "dead" unburied and unmourned in the field when circumstances, stemming from operational setbacks or congressional action, caused America's spies to be abandoned:

> In 1982, someone pasted on the wall of the Central American Task Force the "Six Phases of a U.S. Government Sponsored Covert Action: Enthusiasm—Disillusionment—Panic—Search for the Guilty—Punishment of the Innocent—Praise and Honor for the Nonparticipants." For many in the CIA during the last decade, this is truth.[8]

How had this situation come about? In the case to which Clarridge was making reference, the U.S. Congress had registered its objection to President Ronald Reagan's covert action plan to oppose the Sandinista government in Nicaragua in the early 1980s by first passing a law forbidding the provision of covert aid to the contra opposition "solely for the purpose of overthrowing the Sandinista Government in Nicaragua." Apart from the fact that Congress was legislating openly to restrict an action in which the United States was working hard to deny its participation, the first so-called Boland Amendment did not overly restrict CIA-sponsored covert activities, because it could be argued that the aid was intended primarily to prohibit transshipment of Communist arms through Nicaragua to Communist rebels in El Salvador. However, after the U.S. was shown to have placed firecracker mines at the entrance to Nicaraguan ports in the Caribbean in 1984, in violation of international law and allegedly without notifying its congressional overseers as required by law, the fat was in the fire. An angry Congress passed a second Boland Amendment cutting off all "lethal" aid to the contras, thereby decimating the by now quite overt contra resistance program against the Sandinista government.

Depending on one's point of view, one can lay responsibility for this betrayal of intelligence operatives in the field at the feet of meddling overseers in the opposition party, in the legislative branch of the U.S. government; or blame it on the bungling of the executive branch in not ensuring that Congress understood what was planned for the Nicaraguan harbors. To do either, however, one has to go back in time to see how the legislative branch forced its way into oversight of the spy business in response to the trauma suffered by the spy bureaucracies, especially the CIA, in the early 1970s.

Ramparts magazine, the *New York Times,* and the CIA's internal report on the unearthing of "the family jewels" in 1973–1975 provoked an outburst of public disgust, revulsion, and outrage when they revealed that in the years following World War II, in response to directions from the president and the National Security Council to help "contain" and then roll back the spread of Soviet power, using whatever methods were available, the CIA and the FBI had engaged in a wide range of illegal acts against U.S. citizens and foreign leaders. The spy bureaucracies regularly infiltrated and surveilled domestic anti–Vietnam War groups and some civil rights protesters;

opened the mail of U.S. citizens going to the Soviet Union and Soviet Bloc; supported and paid for the travel to international conferences of the National Student Association; formulated assassination plots against such foreign leaders as Castro, Patrice Lumumba, and Salvador Allende; and supplied mind-altering, hallucinogenic drugs to unsuspecting U.S. subjects.

The reactions to these revelations went on for several years, leading to comprehensive presidential and congressional investigations, the drafting of legislation to limit the activities of the spy bureaucracies, and the promulgation of an executive order by President Gerald Ford governing their conduct. However, the most significant change brought about by this earthquake was that oversight of the spy bureaucracies by the legislative branch of government in the United States was institutionalized. Although the phenomenon of legislative oversight was not copied in the United Kingdom, Israel, or the Soviet Union, its impact was nonetheless felt in these and other countries.

For the first time since the second-oldest profession came into existence, one contemplated a situation where the "need to know" had been expanded so that its practical application was ludicrous as a device to maintain secrecy. If all 535 members of the U.S. Congress are potentially privy to the details of a sensitive spy operation, how can the operation be called a secret? How can "plausible deniability" be maintained as a fiction?

More revolutionary, however, is the change such legislative oversight brought about in the spy bureaucracy itself. No longer are procedures drafted to maintain secrecy and the chain of command in the executive branch sufficient. They must be expanded to allow for examination by an inherently "outside" authority, one that is responsive to the popular will on a daily basis and is by instinct transparent and open to the media. Because of the constant threat of publicity, it is also less tolerant of mistakes, risk taking, and failures. Perhaps that is the price that the spy bureaucracies must pay to be part of a representative, constitutional democracy, but it is antithetical to the spy business, which must be able to rely upon secrecy and discipline to carry out its mission.

So what are the spy bureaucracies left with if, as they see it, they are unable to practice their trade in the manner necessary to produce results and protect their agents?

Graham Greene answered it one way in *The Human Factor,* when espionage threatens to become the game for the sake of the game. We overhear Sir John Hargreaves, head of British intelligence, querying his chief subordinate, Emmanuel Percival, on the death of Davis, an MI6 operative who has just been *poisoned* by Percival for allegedly leaking classified information. Hargreaves and Percival are having their customary weekly lunch at the Travellers in which the most pressing question often appears to be whether they will drink claret or burgundy and eat salmon or trout. Hargreaves finally observes, after hearing Percival's confession of a youthful dalliance with Communism as a student:

> "I sometimes wonder why you are with us, Emmanuel."
>
> "You've just said it, I grew up. I don't think Communism will work—in the long run—any better than Christianity has done, and I'm not the Crusader type. Capitalism or Communism? Perhaps God is a Capitalist. I want to be on the side most likely to win during my lifetime. Don't look shocked, John. You think I'm a cynic, but I just don't want to waste a lot of time. The side that wins will be able to build the better hospitals, and give more to cancer research—when all this atomic nonsense is abandoned. In the meanwhile I enjoy the game we're all playing. Enjoy. Only enjoy. I don't pretend to be an

enthusiast for God or Marx. Beware of people who believe. They aren't reliable players. All the same one grows to like a good player on the other side of the board—it increases the fun."

"Even if he's a traitor?"

"Oh, traitor—that's an old-fashioned word, John. The player is as important as the game. I wouldn't enjoy the game with a bad player across the table."[9]

Four

Counterintelligence

Unlike Jim Prideaux, Mr. George Smiley was not naturally equipped for hurrying in the rain, least of all at dead of night. . . . Small, podgy, and at best middle-aged, he was by appearance one of London's meek who do not inherit the earth. His legs were short, his gait anything but agile, his dress costly, ill-fitting, and extremely wet. His overcoat, which had a hint of widowhood about it, was of that black loose weave which is designed to retain moisture. Either the sleeves were too long or his arms were too short, for . . . when he wore his mackintosh, the cuffs all but concealed the fingers. For reasons of vanity he wore no hat, believing rightly that hats made him ridiculous. . . . Therefore the rain had formed in fat, unbanishable drops on the thick lenses of his spectacles, forcing him alternately to lower or throw back his head as he scuttled along the pavement that skirted the blackened arcades of Victoria Station.[1]

This picture of John le Carré's antihero George Smiley is as defining of the figure of a spy catcher as Sir Arthur Conan Doyle's double-billed cap and pipe for master detective Sherlock

Holmes. Smiley is so unprepossessing that observers literally fail to take note of him. He melts into crowds. As his great friend retired Special Branch Inspector Mendel notes, "You thought, to look at him, that he couldn't cross the road alone, but you might as well have offered protection to a hedgehog."[2]

Smiley is the retired British intelligence officer called back to turn the Circus upside down to find the mole who its present leaders believe has penetrated deep into the Service, in what many critics believe is le Carré's finest pure spy novel, *Tinker, Tailor, Soldier, Spy.*

In fact, *Tinker, Tailor* and much of le Carré's other spy fiction is about *counterintelligence,* as distinguished from "the collection of secret information from foreign countries by illegal means"—Philby's definition of positive, offensive espionage. Smiley's job is to identify and catch the mole who has penetrated British intelligence at the instruction of the Soviet intelligence service and Karla. To accomplish this, Smiley must pore over Circus records and carefully analyze the message traffic and operational security employed during the entire period in which London believes it has been losing spies and spy operations. He must also find a way to interview every individual who has had any meaningful involvement with the cases which have been lost, without alerting them to his mission or scaring them into silence, because he possesses no more authority than his reputation for probity. In short, counterintelligence *is* detective work, but of a highly specialized kind, focusing on operational detail in a secret world where meetings are arranged and held, and messages and intelligence information are exchanged, in a way meant to conceal the fact that they have ever occurred. CI is defensive; it is a way of thinking and seeing; it is the glass half empty, the ability to view the dark side of the moon.

And it is *not* for James Bond or Tom Rogers or Tom Clancy's Jack Ryan.

Each morning as he got out of bed, each evening as he went back to it, usually alone, he had reminded himself that he never was and never had been indispensable. He had schooled himself to admit that in those last wretched months of Control's career, when disasters followed one another with heady speed, he had been guilty of seeing things out of proportion. And if the old professional Adam rebelled in him now and then, and said: You *know* the place went bad, you *know* Jim Prideaux was betrayed—and what more eloquent testimony is there than a bullet, two bullets, in the back? Well, he had replied, suppose he did? And suppose he was right? "It is sheer vanity to believe that one fat middle-aged spy is the only person capable of holding the world together," he would tell himself. And other times: "I never heard of anyone yet who left the Circus without some unfinished business."[3]

So George Smiley would take off his Coke bottle–lensed spectacles and polish them with the thick end of his necktie and remember the counsel of his tutor at Oxford: "Learn the facts, Steed-Asprey used to say, then try on the stories like clothes."[4]

Smiley's quest eventually led him to Bill Haydon and, in *Smiley's People*, to Karla, the remarkable Soviet spymaster who ran Haydon.

In the real world there was no Smiley who tracked down Philby or Burgess or Maclean or Blunt or George Blake. Rather, it was a combination of good counterintelligence investigative work *and* information from independent sources who themselves were either Western penetrations of the Soviet intelligence service or defectors.

For this is the reality of spy catching. Regardless of safeguards installed to vet spies, whether technical, such as the polygraph, or analytical, such as regular and thorough background investigations, there will always be penetration agents, or "moles," who slip through any screen devised by man. That is why competent spy bureaucracies are always on the lookout to recruit spy penetrations of opposing intelligence services and, if the truth be told, of allied services as well. In this fashion, they hope to insulate themselves from traitors in their own ranks by acquiring an informant in the opposing service.

In *Agents of Innocence,* Frank Hoffman's agent quotes a saying of the Prophet Mohammed:

> "A simple Bedouin in the desert asks the Prophet: 'Should I let my camel loose and trust in God?'
> "'No,' says the Prophet. 'Tie down your camel and trust in God.'"[5]

This speaks to the principle that in the world of espionage there are no friendly intelligence services, only those that have not yet been penetrated.

Richard Helms, who served as director of central intelligence under Presidents Lyndon B. Johnson and Richard M. Nixon and was an Agency career official, often remarked during his lifetime that his greatest fear as director was that he would return to his office one day to learn that the CIA had been penetrated. In the end, nothing can be done to protect against that eventuality with absolute certainty.

Nonetheless, Helms was not thinking about a sloppy spy like Aldrich Ames when he admitted to this fear.

Ames was a thirty-year employee of the CIA who, in two meetings with his Russian case officer at the Soviet embassy in Washington, D.C., in April and June 1985, betrayed *every* active espionage and counterintelligence operation that the United States was running against the Soviet Union at the time.

His treachery permitted the Soviets to catch and execute at least ten Soviet spies working for the U.S. and probably several more. In addition, over the period in which he spied for the Russians, Ames revealed to them the names of scores of U.S. intelligence officers; the gaps in CIA knowledge about the U.S.S.R.; the techniques the CIA, the FBI, and other U.S. intelligence organizations used to collect intelligence about them; and what our targets in the Soviet Union were. Along with the case of convicted FBI spy Robert P. Hanssen, Ames's was one of the most significant betrayals the United States had ever suffered at the hands of one of its own spies.

Ames was arrested on February 22, 1994, so his spying went on for nine years. The enormity of the losses to U.S. intelligence due to Ames's betrayal were already manifest in 1986, raising the question of why it had taken so long for the U.S. to catch him, particularly since Ames took few precautions to protect his own security.

Ames was paid more than $4 million for his treachery, and he spent the money lavishly. He paid cash for his house in Arlington, Virginia; spent $30,000 plus in credit card expenditures per month; remodeled his house; bought two Jaguar automobiles during this period; had his teeth fixed; bought new clothes; and traveled extensively, all on a midlevel government salary.

In addition, he was a chronic alcohol abuser. He was often drunk in public and on the job, collapsing in the streets of Mexico City and Rome after embassy functions, arguing uncontrollably with a Cuban diplomat at an embassy reception, leaving his wallet and operational notes at a joint FBI-CIA picnic, and frequently falling asleep in his CIA office after a boozy lunch.

Finally, Ames was highly irregular in the conduct of his spy duties. He was chronically late in filing reports on his meetings with Soviet officials who were potential targets for recruitment, so-called contact reports. In some instances he failed to file them at all, which drew complaints from the FBI that were never pursued by Ames's CIA supervisors. He also failed to complete on time his financial accountings for operational expenses and travel, a significant oversight in an organization that can expend large sums of money on the mere signature of one of its employees.

When the CIA slowly and ponderously cranked up its inadequately staffed mole-hunting team to try to find out in 1987 how the U.S. government had lost all of its reporting assets against its most important intelligence target in the space of a few months, why wasn't Aldrich Ames an obvious candidate? He had had access to all of the case files that had been betrayed, and he was a ranking counterintelligence expert in Soviet affairs.

The answer is both general and specific. First, the CIA had been penetrated previously by serving staff officers: Larry Wu-Tai Chin had spied for the Chinese for thirty-three years and been caught in the 1970s; William Kampiles had sold the KH-11 satellite manual to the Russians from his position in the operations center of the CIA during the same time period; and Edward Lee Howard had revealed operations and the names of agency personnel in the CIA station in Moscow to the Soviets in an act of revenge for having been summarily dismissed from the Agency for substance abuse in the early 1980s. Nevertheless, there had never been a spy penetration case of this magnitude at CIA before, one that involved a blue-badged career staff officer who had passed periodic polygraph reexaminations, as Ames had.

Second, even though Ames drove a Jaguar and lived well, his new girlfriend and soon-to-be wife was a well-born Colombian, and he had implied that she was the source of his new wealth. Furthermore, there were lots of luxury cars in the CIA parking lot and not all of them were driven by traitors.

Third, there were many spy runners in the Directorate of

Operations (DO) who had alcohol abuse problems, some far worse than Ames's, and that did not signify that they were spies.

Fourth, although Ames had had access to all of the Soviet cases which were betrayed, so had a good many other DO officers, and in the early handicapping, Ames wasn't even the prime suspect. A former deputy director for operations, then inspector general, had looked at the betrayed cases and pronounced that they had all had security vulnerabilities of one sort or another—"the seeds of their own destruction," he called them.

Finally, counterintelligence lore was well settled in the Directorate of Operations. To break a CI case, one needed independent source information, preferably a penetration of the other side's intelligence organization. In other words, no matter how scrupulous the analysis by the mole hunters, exhaustive detective work alone would not get you there. One needed a penetration of the Soviet intelligence service or a defector, a volunteer, to come forward to identify the mole.

As appealing as these rationalizations may be, they fail to explain the counterintelligence disaster that the Ames case represented for the CIA and U.S. intelligence.

In the first place, one had only to visit CIA Headquarters at the time of Ames's betrayal to sense a complete lack of counterintelligence consciousness. The Agency had grown by nearly 30 percent during the buildup of the William Casey–Ronald Reagan years and acted and reacted like a mature bureaucracy. Walking the halls was more like visiting the Department of Agriculture than visiting the world's premier spy organization. More attention was paid to the guest musicians playing in the employees' courtyard outside the Agency cafeteria during July Fourth celebrations than to a CIA employee carrying out eight-inch stacks of classified information in a book bag.

Counterintelligence was not "in," either as a career or as a concern, in the early 1990s. James Jesus Angleton had been the counterintelligence maven at the CIA from its creation until 1975 and had been in the job too long. His paranoia about a Soviet penetration of the Agency had paralyzed Soviet operations for a decade. Angleton's excesses at the end of his career had spoiled the appeal of counterintelligence as a career for twenty years after his departure, and CIA employees had become just as concerned about and protective of their right to privacy as any other group of Americans. Few employees believed that they were in fact their brother's keeper on security issues, even if they observed the rules being obviously flouted. Except in the more sensitive precincts of the Directorate of Operations, there was little conscious recognition that the spy business was different and had stricter requirements of "need to know" and compartmentation. Even in the DO, discipline had broken down in the aftermath of the end of the Cold War. As Ames learned to his profit, Russian area spy runners were not reluctant to discuss current "cases" with an old Soviet hand in the headquarters courtyard over a smoke after lunch.

Moreover, as Paul Redmond, America's version of George Smiley (and a profane, brash, outspoken, caustic, courageous one at that) often remarks, "Americans are just too *nice* to do counterintelligence well." They're not *nasty* enough, says Redmond, to grasp the implications of an Ames betrayal and follow the investigative trail relentlessly, single-mindedly, and perhaps brutally to a conclusion. Redmond also notes that most good spy runners stay away from the counterintelligence field because it's a downer. It always brings *bad* news, and senior officials get tired of hearing the grisly details from CI officers and begin to equate the messenger with the message.

Indeed, in explaining the U.S. reaction to Ames, Redmond takes his criticism one step further: "In addition to not liking the espionage and the counterespionage business and what it requires, Americans are sort of naïve and there's a bit of moral ambiguity in a lot of us."[6]

The United States can be thankful for Paul Redmond's persistence in the Ames case. He and his mole-hunting team, with some pauses and detours, persevered in their effort to explain the devastating losses of 1985 and tracked Ames through two repolygraphs that he had ostensibly passed, an effort which would have daunted less diligent folk.

Finally, in explanation of the long hunt for Ames, the CIA was afflicted by its own version of Murphy's Law. Everything that could have gone wrong with an investigation of this nature did go wrong. A colleague of Ames's in Mexico City in the 1980s, Diana Worthen, knew that he had no money and neither did his new girlfriend, Rosario Casas. Worthen was overwhelmed by Ames's unexplained new wealth, and when she returned to Headquarters she reported the fact to counterintelligence authorities in 1990, well before Ames's scheduled periodic re-polygraph in 1991. Somehow the memorandum containing Worthen's observations never made it to the Office of Security and the polygraph examiners for use in questioning Ames.

Likewise, a superb field background investigation was conducted on Ames prior to the 1991 repolygraph which caught all the issues: Ames's conspicuous wealth and lavish spending, his alcohol abuse, and his penchant for being late in his financial accountings and contact reports. Yet this background reinvestigation report was not considered by the polygrapher before Ames was examined, and Ames was not pressed for explanations on the issues, even though the examination clearly detected weaknesses in his responses to questions about contact with foreign nationals.

For a long time the polygraph has been the object of false advertising by CIA. The fiction was always maintained that the polygraph was but one tool in the vetting of applicants for CIA employment and retention, and the Agency looked at "the whole person" in assessing employability. The polygraph results were supposedly coupled with the findings of the full field background investigation, and, if the employee was already on board, his reputation on the job and his previous performance, to make the complete security assessment. In point of fact, the polygraph was determinative of a security clearance. Despite the knowledge that it is more of an art than a science, that it regularly produces false positives and negatives, and that it is highly dependent on the skill and experience of the operator, no CIA security professional would grant a clearance to an applicant or recommend the retention of one if the applicant or employee "failed" the polygraph examination. The individual's reputation or background examination would never override a negative polygraph—that was the bureaucratic reality. As a consequence, in the 1980s and early 1990s, before Ames was arrested, polygraphers bent over backward to get examinees, especially existing employees, through the polygraph. In an ironic and totally inappropriate reflection of the consumer focus of the time, examinees were even asked to fill out a customer-satisfaction form about the polygraph interview—as if it ever should or could be a "satisfying" consumer experience.

America's passion for technology, which made it so successful in other aspects of espionage, was unrequited when it came to the polygraph in many counterintelligence situations. Ames might have been pursued more single-mindedly had the preparations for his 1986 and 1991 polygraph examinations been more thorough and the tests administered more at arm's length. It is a further reason to applaud the diligence and persistence of Paul Redmond's mole hunters, who forged ahead and confronted Ames in the face of his positive polygraph results.

Apart from the questions surrounding Ames's polygraphs, however, the verdict on U.S. counterintelligence competence in the Ames affair must be quite severe. It is difficult to explain, much less justify, how an officer with a mediocre operational track record, an alcohol abuse problem, and a reputation for filing late accountings and contact reports could be on the CIA's first team for meeting and assessing Soviet embassy officials for potential recruitment as U.S. spies. Aldrich Ames belonged on the loading dock, not on the flight line.

Similar observations can be made about the FBI's ineptitude in tracking Robert P. Hanssen. Throughout the course of his treachery, there was no effort to compartment his access to the FBI's most sensitive CI and espionage cases because his information technology skills were superb and in high demand. Furthermore, although America's spy agencies place a greater burden on the polygraph to uncover spies than the machine can deliver, the FBI did not even repolygraph its senior officials on a regular basis prior to or after the Ames debacle.

Five

Tradecraft

And his fancy that he was being followed?
What of that? What of the shadow he never saw,
only felt, till his back seemed to tingle with the
intensity of his watcher's gaze; he saw nothing, heard
nothing, only felt. He was too old not to heed the
warning. The creak of a stair that had not creaked
before; the rustle of a shutter when no wind was
blowing; the car with a different number plate but
the same scratch on the offside wing; the face on the
Metro that you know you have seen somewhere
before: for years at a time these were signs he had
lived by; any one of them was reason enough to
move, change towns, identities. For in that profession there is no such thing as coincidence.[1]

The techniques adopted by spies to conceal their activities are
lumped together under the catch-all term "tradecraft." It refers
to a vast range of protective measures devised to preserve the
operational security of spying: " 'If there's one thing that distinguishes a good watcher from a bad one,' said Jim, 'it's the gentle
art of doing damn all convincingly.' "[2]
    The literature is filled with examples of astonishing trade-
craft. Charles de Gaulle's fictional assassin M. Chacal creates

three separate identities to get close to his intended target in Frederick Forsyth's *The Day of the Jackal*.[3] The following reference to a Czech message code enables Jack Brotherhood in John le Carré's *A Perfect Spy* to figure out why Magnus Pym is always seeking old numbers of the local newspapers in which to wrap his spy films:

> "Sure. There's two ways. One way they use the day of the month, the other way they use the day of the week. Day of the month is a nightmare: thirty-one standard messages to be learned by heart. It's the eighteenth of the month so it's 'Meet me behind the gentleman's convenience in Brno at nine-thirty and don't be late.' It's the sixth so 'Where the hell's my monthly pay cheque?' "[4]

Maurice Castle in Graham Greene's *The Human Factor* uses a book code to communicate with his Soviet control, through a bookstore owned by a longtime Communist Party member in Charing Cross. Mr. Verloc in Joseph Conrad's *The Secret Agent* communicates by changing the display of wares in his shop window.[5]

"Survival . . . is an infinite capacity for suspicion," notes the nearly assassinated Jim Prideaux in *Tinker, Tailor, Soldier, Spy*, because, as le Carré concludes in the same novel, "Treason is very much a matter of habit."[6] The spy must live the legend he has constructed for himself. Any deviation may open him to detection and apprehension.

Sound tradecraft is, if anything, more important in the real world of espionage. If it had not been for the ceaseless efforts of Pyotr Popov's case officer, George Kisevalter, Popov would have compromised himself with his operational carelessness early in his career of spying for the West. Popov failed to distance himself from his Serbian girlfriend even after his wife

PYOTR POPOV
The peasant risen to officer rank in the GRU, the Soviet military intelligence service, who supplied the West with valuable order-of-battle and personnel information about the U.S.S.R., at great risk to his own security, from important positions in Vienna and Berlin during the 1950s.

became pregnant. He took enormous risks in carrying out reams of Soviet military intelligence in broad daylight from Soviet offices in Central Vienna. He constantly forgot his regular and emergency recontact telephone numbers, so his U.S. handlers had to track him down from open travel listings. His behavior illustrated a chronic weakness in spy operations. The spy becomes so blinded by his hatred for the country he is spying on (Popov) or so confident of his ability to fool everyone (Ames and Penkovsky) that he takes enormous personal risks.

Aldrich Ames became very cavalier about his tradecraft, and it is surprising that his Russian spymasters did not jack him up more often in order to prolong the life of the operation. He often turned up inebriated, at meetings with his Soviet control, and several times became so befuddled that he forgot the city appointed for his next rendezvous, once appearing in Vienna when he was supposed to be in Zurich. In addition, he occasionally stuffed classified information in his checked luggage en route to or from spy meetings. At the end of one such trip to Latin America, toward the end of his escapades, he was caught in a telephone conversation taped by the FBI being chewed out by his wife, Rosario, in "expletives deleted" language, for his operational stupidity.

Finally, in one of the last trips before his arrest, Ames stored classified spy information in the laptop computer he was sharing with his Agency supervisor on an official trip to an international conference in Turkey. How he proposed to explain to his colleague the existence of this classified data on the machine was never made clear, since by that time the CIA and the FBI were closing in on him and his colleague was witting of his betrayal.

Robert Hanssen does not appear to have been as careless as Ames. During the fifteen years of his treachery, he never met his Russian control. He took great pains to conceal his real identity from the Russians. He alone selected the hiding places, or "dead drops," where he concealed the spy information he was providing them and received the cash in payment. He attempted to live a frugal life, with a modest house in the Virginia suburbs, an old car, and unfashionable clothes. There are some odd wrinkles that have since come out about his friendship with a prostitute and his showering of gifts upon her, which would have endangered his operational security had it become known, but it does not appear that this altered his visible lifestyle.

Nonetheless, it is clear that tradecraft or operational security is a practice that constantly needs reinforcement in the real world of espionage. The reason why is not difficult to explain. Tradecraft practices add enormous amounts of planning and time to even the simplest clandestine meeting or information pass. Kisevalter and his associates spent days planning for the next meeting and debriefing of both Popov and Penkovsky. They were constantly concerned that overexposure of these prime assets to Westerners in general, and to the clandestine brush contact in Penkovsky's case in particular, would draw the attention of the counterintelligence arm of the KGB. And they were right to be worried. It is nearly impossible to describe adequately the hostility of the environment that existed in the Soviet Union and Soviet Bloc countries during the Cold War period toward normal intercourse between Soviet citizens and Westerners, much less brush passes and loading and unloading dead drops. "Moscow Rules," as le Carré dubbed them in Smiley's contest with Karla, were standard procedure and de rigueur for operating successfully in the Bloc.

One of the principal reasons why the West had so few recruitments of Soviet spies during the early years of the Cold War was that meaningful contact between Western intelligence officers and Soviet targets was next to nonexistent, or at best tightly controlled and observed. This was as true outside the Soviet Bloc as it was inside, since the Soviets brought their counterintelligence apparatus out with them, to their embassies and consulates in the West. Unless a spy possessed the determination and good fortune of a Popov or a Penkovsky, a clandestine arrangement could never be forged in the way Clarridge pursued Adamski in Turkey.

The cumbersomeness of tradecraft precautions affected covert action operations as well, given the aim of preserving the "plausible deniability" upon which the National Security Council and Presidents Dwight D. Eisenhower and John F. Kennedy insisted during the heyday of covert actions in the 1950s and early 1960s. It was most inefficient and time-consuming to plan an amphibious landing in Cuba when the materiel had to be World War II vintage, obtainable on the open arms market, and the training had to be largely offshore and could not involve American personnel in the invasion force. Of course it turned out to be ineffective and self-defeating as well, since regular U.S. forces were not turned loose to prevent disaster in the Bay of Pigs, and nobody believed that it was not a U.S. operation anyway.

Far more insidious for successful spy operations, however, is the breakdown in tradecraft that has taken place on occasion at the CIA, during the waning days of the Cold War and since. In the mid-1980s, the CIA was reported to have lost, in one blow, almost twenty spies reporting from an important Middle Eastern adversary. The spies were apparently sending out their messages by letter to a common address (called an "accommodation address") in Europe, but the cover text that concealed their reports in secret writing appeared to have been drafted by one person with a distinctive hand whom the target country's counterintelligence authorities were able to identify, because the procedure had been in use without change for so long. The authorities quickly rounded up the spies.

In 1995, in a flap in Paris during a French presidential election, French newspapers reported that reputed CIA spy runners were meeting French officials from sensitive government departments when the Americans knew or should have known that they were under surveillance by the French internal security service. In addition, spy meetings were reportedly being set up from open official telephone lines rather than public call boxes, to save time. In similar fashion, the French press reported surveillance avoidance routes were being cut short to save time, and some agent meetings were taking place in well-known hotels too close to the center of Paris, where the French counterintelligence service could observe the meetings. French government sources released their version of the episode to the French media with the express purpose of embarrassing the U.S. government.

This sloppiness in tradecraft practices appears to have stemmed from the mistaken notions that Paris was a "friendly" environment for espionage operations; that the French had better things to do than worry whether the United States was spying on them, since the French themselves were busy spying on visiting U.S. businessmen; and that even if the United States was caught out, the matter would be handled discreetly, on an intelligence-service-to-intelligence-service basis. Wrong! The point is, tradecraft still matters even if the totalitarian control of Soviet society that gave rise to Moscow Rules during the Cold War has disappeared. Successful espionage is impossible without tight operational security.

The events of September 11, 2001, underscore this admonition. There were nineteen Arab men who hijacked the aircraft that struck the World Trade Center towers and the Pentagon and crashed in the field near Shankstown, Pennsylvania. They were professionals, for the most part, without previous terrorist involvement, from so-called moderate Arab allies of the United States, i.e., Saudi Arabia, Egypt, and the United Arab Emirates. They maintained tight operational discipline over a long period preparatory to the attacks. Some of them lived in the United States with their families during the two years prior to 9/11, keeping to themselves, going to flight school, and nobody came forward to report any suspicious behavior. It is still unclear whether all of them knew that their 9/11 mission entailed suicide, but they were remarkably discreet in their movements, and the organization that funded their preparations was highly sophisticated.

If this sets the standard for operational security for future terrorist attacks in the West, Al Qaeda or otherwise, then an equally careful and professional standard of operational technique will be required to defeat them. U.S. and allied law enforcement and intelligence agencies will have to be alert to all of the sophisticated spy methodology made possible by the information technology revolution embodied in the Internet, cell phones, and electronic funds transfers—the accoutrements of globalization.

Six

Heroes

In the spy world, one country's hero is another's villain. This chapter will focus on those spies and spy runners who made enormous contributions to intelligence gathering in the West, especially during the Cold War.

To begin, however, I will examine the literary antecedents. As noted earlier, the first generation of spy novels featured the protagonist as spy hero, or, in the case of Mr. Verloc in Conrad's *The Secret Agent,* villain. "Some of the highest in the world got to thank me for walking on their two legs today," says Verloc to the imperious czarist diplomat to whom he has been reporting anarchist plots as a paid agent.[1]

In response to his control's command to produce "a series of outrages,"[2] Verloc hatches a plot to blow up the Greenwich Observatory. To place the bomb, he involves his half-witted brother-in-law, who in the act unexpectedly stumbles and falls, detonating the device and blowing himself to smithereens. At this point, the real hero steps forward—Verloc's wife, Winnie, who is the spy's antithesis: "Curiosity being one of the forms of self-revelation, a systematically incurious person remains always partly mysterious."[3] Winnie's watchword is "Things do not stand much looking into."[4]

Winnie has been perfectly willing to live with this obese, lazy lump of a "revolutionary-manqué" husband and provider, on the strength of his willingness to tolerate her live-in mother and brother Stevie, but when Verloc supplies the instrument for Stevie's death in pursuit of Mr. Vladimir's wish for "activity," she is driven to revenge her brother. Winnie stabs Verloc to death as he reclines on their couch; then she seeks to escape to the Continent. Conrad's view appears to be that this entire world of anarchist plotting, demonstrations, and bomb making at the turn of the twentieth century is unreal and meaningless posturing, except as it may spill over and accidentally affect innocent lives like those of Stevie and Winnie, at which point Winnie's outraged vengeful act becomes the only touch of reality in this spy universe.

This is emphatically not the case in the spying of Davies and Carruthers in *The Riddle of the Sands,* by Erskine Childers. There, Davies is on a quest to show that at the dawn of the twentieth century, with no North Sea fleet or shore defense on the East Anglian coast, England stands vulnerable to an attack by the Kaiser's Germany through the sand berms that dot the lonely stretch of Frisian coast between Holland and Denmark. Davies is an eccentric, a summertime sailor who has often cruised this region. He believes the Germans will accomplish their invasion with an armada of small boats, whose buildup the slumbering British admiralty will not detect until it is too late, unless he and Carruthers fully scout the German preparations themselves and report on it directly. After narrowly escaping drowning at the hands of a man named Dollmann whom he suspects of being an English spy *for* the Germans, Davies discusses his mission with his shipmate Carruthers:

> "There *must* be more to find out than the mere navigation of those channels, and if that's so, mightn't we come to be genuine spies ourselves?"
>
> "And, after all, hang it!" exclaimed Davies, "if it comes to that, why shouldn't we? I look at it like this.

The man's an Englishman, and if he's in with Germany he's a traitor to us, and we as Englishmen have a right to expose him. If we can't do it without spying we've a right to spy, at our own risk—"

"There's a stronger argument than that. He tried to take your life."

"I don't care a rap about that. I'm not such an ass as to thirst for revenge and all that, like some chap in a shilling shocker. But it makes me wild to think of that fellow masquerading as a German, and up to who knows what mischief—mischief enough to make him want to get rid of *any* one. I'm keen about the sea, and I think they're apt to be a bit slack at home," he continued inconsequently. "Those Admiralty chaps want waking up. . . ."[5]

In short, it's Dollmann's treachery that supplies part, but not all, of Davies's motivation. Davies has a good geopolitical grasp of the situation, as good spies or spy runners should:

"I don't blame them," said Davies, who, for all his patriotism, had not a particle of racial spleen in his composition. "I don't blame them; their Rhine ceases to be German just when it begins to be most valuable. The mouth is Dutch, and would give them magnificent ports just opposite British shores. We can't talk about conquest and grabbing. We've collared a fine share of the world, and they've every right to be jealous. Let them hate us, and say so; it'll teach us to buck up; and that's what really matters." . . .

To be thrown with Davies was to receive a shock of enlightenment; for here, at least, was a specimen of the breed who exacted respect. It is true he made use of the usual jargon, interlarding his stammering sentences (sometimes, when he was excited, with the oddest effect) with the conventional catchwords of the journalist and platform speaker. But these were but accidents; for he seemed to have caught his innermost conviction from the very soul of the sea itself. An armchair critic is one thing, but a sun-burnt, brine-burnt zealot smarting under a personal discontent, athirst for a means, however tortuous, of contributing his effort to the great cause, the mar-itime supremacy of Britain, that was quite another thing. He drew inspiration from the very wind and spray. He communed with his tiller, I believe, and marshaled his figures with its help. To hear him talk was to feel a current of clarifying air blustering into a close club-room, where men bandy ineffectual plat-itudes, and mumble old shibboleths, and go away and do nothing.[6]

This inspiration causes Davies to perform the most remark-able feat of navigating and endurance, dead-reckoning a small rowing skiff through pea-soup fog on a twenty-mile round trip to Memmert from Norderney, to enable Carruthers to over-hear the Germans pursue preparations for the invasion of Britain. And when the mission is accomplished and Carruthers has to return to London to report for duty to his superior at the Foreign Office, the two amateurs recognize that they have been learning the skills of the spy trade:

> "Carruthers! What are we talking about? If they [the Germans] have the ghost of a notion where we have been today, you give us away by packing off to Lon-don. They'll think we know their secret and are

clearing out to make use of it. *That* means arrest, if you like!"

"Pessimist! Haven't I written proof of good faith in my pocket—official letters of recall, received today? It's one deception the less, you see; for those letters *may* have been opened; skillfully done it's impossible to detect. When in doubt, tell the truth!"

"It's a rum thing how often it pays in this spying business," said Davies, thoughtfully.[7]

Spying had thus become the medium for a first-rate adventure story, with, in Childers's case, a ring of authenticity which caused the British government to look hard at its coastal defenses after his novel was published. *The Riddle of the Sands* was followed by John Buchan's *The Thirty-nine Steps,* which was written just prior to World War I and featured the adventures of another volunteer spy hero. Richard Hannay is a colonial, from Rhodesia, who after confessing to boredom in summertime London is drawn haplessly into a murder, and in short order becomes a suspect. He flees to Scotland and embarks upon a picaresque series of impersonations and narrow escapes until he is drawn back into the web of the real murderer, a man who can "hood his eyes like a hawk."[8] This man is in fact a German involved in a scheme, called the Black Stone, designed to draw Britain into a Balkan war after the assassination of a prominent Greek politician on British soil and after the Germans have stolen the joint Franco-British war plans for the region.

Hannay is a remarkable if wholly untutored spy who helps deduce the location of the Black Stone plotters on the English coast and walks in on them accusingly, without a shred of evidence to support his theory except his recollection of the hawk-like hooded eyes of the leader. However, he expostulates on the nature of disguise in words destined for the spy tradecraft hall of fame. After noting the difficulty of making a positive identification in differing circumstances, he wisely concludes: "A fool tries to look different; a clever man looks the same but *is* different."[9]

Real-life spy heroes don't look or act like Winnie Verloc, Davies and Carruthers, or Richard Hannay. They are more like Pyotr Popov, a volunteer with woman troubles, a peasant with a grudge against the Soviet system. Popov spied for the West from 1952 to 1958, taking extraordinary risks to bring out Soviet order-of-battle military secrets and make possible the identification of hundreds of Soviet KGB (civilian intelligence) and GRU (military intelligence) officers and illegals (Soviet spies with manufactured identities destined for service in the West). He appears to have become fed up with the lying and hypocrisy of the Soviet system, but he himself was a remarkable Russian success story. It was most unusual for a peasant to make his way from the enlisted ranks to officer status and, after a solid but uninspiring war record, to the prestigious M. V. Frunze Military Academy after World War II. Nonetheless, by the time Popov arrived in Vienna in 1951, his career had probably topped out. His German-language skills were poor, confining him to lesser espionage targets, and he had become involved with a Serbian mistress, getting her pregnant. It was the pregnancy that triggered his call for help and offer to spy, contained in a message dropped in the parked car of an American diplomat.

Actually, the real hero of the Popov case was his case officer, the CIA official whose primary responsibility was to debrief Popov and guide him to the secrets the U.S. wanted him to steal, but critically also to watch over Popov's tradecraft and keep the relationship operationally secure. George Kisevalter was Popov's handler or case officer. In the opinion of many of his colleagues, Kisevalter was possessed of a Russian soul, and he empathized, inspired, scolded, and counseled Popov throughout his spying career for the West. Kisevalter spoke Russian fluently, having worked with Russian soldiers as a liaison during World War II.

It is difficult to define with precision the requirements for a successful spy runner, but a liking for the culture in which one operates and a profound understanding of human nature are clearly two. And in most cases, the character one has to understand is *foreign,* with its own prejudices and neuroses. There was a subtle disconnect in the beginning of the Popov operation, which illustrates this point, when Popov was first met by an American case officer of Russian extraction who had recently emigrated from the Soviet Union. Popov nearly abandoned his espionage enterprise, because he knew how completely the KGB had penetrated the émigré community, and he had no trust in this newly minted American, even though he obviously spoke perfect Russian. Kisevalter turned out to be the ideal contact because he understood most of Popov's hangups and weaknesses, and could anticipate his needs and his failings. Running spies is far more complex than setting collection requirements and receiving raw intelligence information in exchange for money. It often entails getting into the head and guts of the recruited spy.

As to the desirability of understanding a foreign culture, Dewey Clarridge expresses it well in his autobiography, speaking of India:

> Many Westerners who serve there get hung up on the bone-crunching poverty of India, the filth and the flies and the begging. After a short time, I was uncritical of what I saw and felt no compulsion to change anything. To me there was so much beauty and fascination in the people and the country that the squalor paled. Although even today I cannot

account for it, I never felt like an outsider during my stay in the subcontinent.[10]

In the event, Popov was probably betrayed by George Blake, a British SIS officer who became aware of Popov's existence when the latter reestablished contact with U.S. intelligence by hailing two British military attachés in East Germany, after having been on ice during a sojourn in Moscow. Blake was a KGB penetration of British intelligence who revealed a number of crucial Western secrets to the Soviets, including the existence of the Berlin Tunnel. Yet Popov had taken enormous risks in spying for the West, despite Kisevalter's constant efforts to save him from himself. It was almost as if, having made up his mind not to submit any longer to the tyranny of the Soviet state, he did not care if he got caught.

William Hood, in *Mole,* captures Kisevalter's predicament in handling a sensitive agent like Popov. Popov has just announced to Kisevalter (who bears the name Domnin in Hood's fictionalized account) that, despite Kisevalter's continual instruction to the contrary, Popov is still in contact with his Serbian mistress, Lyuba:

> Domnin [Kisevalter] was angry and depressed. Popov had been in contact with CIA for four years. As far as Domnin could know, there had been no security breaks on the CIA side. The agency had taken every possible precaution in disseminating Popov's material—it had been attributed to a variety of notional sources and never pinpointed as coming from an in-place agent or originating in Austria. Scores of reports had been disseminated, some so sensitive they had been sent under an *Eyes Only* rubric to the White House and the secretaries of state and defense. Even after four years, the Popov

BIGOT list showed only a handful of persons were fully informed of the details of the operation.

Despite his GRU training, his experience as a CIA agent, and Domnin's coaching, Popov continued to take avoidable chances and to cut security corners. Only a bull-headed peasant, Domnin thought, would carry on with Lyuba, hand a devastatingly revealing letter to a stranger, and dash across the street to embrace his case officer in public. Popov was stubborn, he reflected, and sentimental as well.

Across the coffee table, Popov was sulking, stung by his case officer's rebuke. . . . "Okay, Pyotr, enough recrimination for today." Domnin smiled. "What else is it you've got on your mind?"

The tension broken, Popov managed a slight smile.[11]

These are, after all, human beings committing espionage— i.e., treason. Despite every effort of the spy runner to think *for* him, the agent is the man on the spot, and he *will* insist on being himself.

Not all the spy operations which were highly successful during the Cold War involved human agents and their case officers. As noted earlier, in 1955 U.S. and British intelligence constructed a tunnel that ran for four hundred yards under the Soviet sector of Berlin to a telephone cable connecting the Soviet high command in East Berlin to the general staff and foreign office in Moscow, and with all Soviet military and official installations in East Germany. The tunnel ran from a mock U.S. Army "radar station" near Rudow, in the American sector, beneath the border separating West from East Berlin. In all, the tunnel was nearly six hundred yards long and six feet high, and it was approximately fifteen feet underground.

The Berlin Tunnel, as it came to be called, was the brain-child of William King Harvey, chief of the CIA's Berlin Operations Base (BOB). It took months to build, by hand, with the prime qualification for spy runners assigned to BOB during this period not necessarily being the number of Soviet recruitment scalps on their belt, but whether they had strong backs and a capacity for hard physical labor.

Harvey was an extraordinary U.S. intelligence officer. Originally a counterintelligence expert with the FBI, he had been the Bureau officer responsible for debriefing Whittaker Chambers, Elizabeth Bentley, and other American Communists who had spied for the Soviets early on and come forward to defect in the late 1930s and 1940s. He was a two-fisted drinker, with a barroom bouncer's girth, who was cowed by nothing and nobody. Allegedly he was the senior U.S. intelligence officer who convinced DCI Walter Bedell Smith to go to the British and demand Kim Philby's recall from Washington after Burgess and Maclean fled to the U.S.S.R. in the early 1950s.

Recognizing the extreme difficulty BOB was experiencing in recruiting Russian spies, Harvey determined to skin the cat another way by eavesdropping on the Soviets' operational communications. The tunnel was his idea, and he pushed it to consummation, getting the British to make the actual tap into the telephone cable. At its peak, the tap gave access to more than 430 telephone lines; conversations were systematically recorded by tape recorders during the more than twelve months the tap was in operation.

It now appears that the tunnel was compromised early in its existence also by George Blake, who was part of the British SIS team privy to construction of the tunnel. Nonetheless, the Soviets permitted the tap to operate for more than thirteen months before Khrushchev closed it down, when the Soviets stumbled over it "accidentally." For a good while after it was concluded that Blake had compromised the operation, it was assumed that the Soviets had altered the communications traffic over the tapped lines from the moment of betrayal. However, according to a remarkable book, *Battleground Berlin,*[12] made possible by cooperation between the Boris Yeltsin government and the United States after the Soviet Union's demise in 1991, it now appears that the Soviets did nothing to alter or disguise their operational traffic over the tapped lines during the period that the tunnel was in business.

Sergei Kondrashev was *Rezident* (chief) of the KGB station in East Germany at Karlshorst at this time. While not ruling out the early assumption that the Soviets might have refrained from taking any counterintelligence action to alter the communications traffic over the tapped lines in order to protect their penetration by Blake, Kondrashev, one of the authors of *Battleground Berlin,* focuses on two different points. He argues that Soviet military commanders and high government officials were expected to communicate sensitive matters over a separate, dedicated landline established for that purpose. In addition, he states that the KGB assumed that the military commanders and senior officials would observe greater communications discipline and would not rattle on about troop movements or sensitive matters over an open line. On these two points, he was overly optimistic. During the period when the tap was in operation, the Western intelligence services harvested a bonanza of useful intelligence information about the Soviets' defense forces, their logistical capabilities, and their plans in the event of hostilities. The intelligence gained also included information about the identities and placement of Soviet intelligence officers in Central Europe.

A more cogent and human explanation for the Soviet decision to do nothing about communications traffic on the tapped cable is that it was just too difficult. To have attempted to get all users of the tapped lines to change their procedures would have been an enormous and insecure undertaking, which doubtless would have raised more questions than could have been speedily answered. Clearly, Khrushchev and the Soviet high command chose to take their chances, rely on operational discipline, and close the tunnel down at a time when suspicion about its betrayal might fall not on a human spy but on the passage of time.

The Berlin Tunnel was a remarkable Cold War spying success story, and it prompted many subsequent efforts at technical penetration by both Eastern and Western spy services, including the recently revealed U.S. effort in the 1980s to construct a tunnel into the new Russian embassy atop Mt. Alto in Washington, D.C. This latter-day tunnel was completed but betrayed by Robert P. Hanssen and never became operational.

> As a boy, Ramius sensed more than thought that Soviet Communism ignored a basic human need. In his teens, his misgivings began to take a coherent shape. The Good of the People was a laudable enough goal, but in denying a man's soul, an enduring part of his being, Marxism stripped away the foundation of human dignity and individual value. It also cast aside the objective measure of justice and ethics which, he decided, was the principal legacy of religion to civilized life. From earliest adulthood on, Marko had his own idea about right and wrong, an idea he did not share with the State. It gave him a means of gauging his actions and those of others. It was something he was careful to conceal. It served as an anchor for his soul and, like an anchor, it was hidden far below the visible surface.[13]

These musings of master skipper and submarine driver Marko Ramius are the prelude to his decision to steal the latest

Soviet ballistic missile submarine, equipped with a revolutionary supersilent, top secret underwater propulsion system called "the caterpillar," from Northern Fleet Headquarters on the Baltic and deliver it to the U.S. Navy in Norfolk, Virginia, in exchange for political asylum for himself and senior members of his crew.

Yet it is not salvation of his soul alone that motivates Ramius in *The Hunt for Red October.* Despite his recognized skills as a seaman and sub driver, he realizes that he will always be suspect to the Great Russian elite who run the U.S.S.R. because of his Lithuanian heritage. He will never be regarded or trusted by the admiralty as 100 percent Russian.

The event which catalyzed his decision to defect was far more bitter and personal, however. Ramius's wife, Natalia, had lost her life to the criminal negligence of a drunken Soviet surgeon who had allowed her inflamed appendix to burst before he could sober up enough to operate on her. Furthermore, she died of peritonitis because the antibiotic used to treat her had been either watered down or stolen by underpaid Soviet medical technicians. In short, the Soviet system was rotten to the core and Ramius wanted out:

> The life of Natalia Bogdanova Ramius had been lost at the hands of a surgeon who had been drinking while on call—a court-martial offense in the Soviet Navy—but Marko could not have the doctor punished. The surgeon was himself the son of a Party chieftain, his status secured by his own sponsors. Her life might have been saved by proper medication, but there had not been enough foreign drugs, and Soviet pharmaceuticals were untrustworthy. The doctor could not be made to pay, the pharmaceutical workers could not be made to pay—the thought echoed back and forth across his mind,

feeding his fury until he decided that the State would be made to pay.[14]

> Ramius looked around the table at his officers. Most had not been allowed to pursue their own career goals despite their proficiency and despite their Party membership. The minor infractions of youth—in one case an act committed at age eight—prevented two from ever being trusted again. With the missile officer, it was because he was a Jew; though his parents had always been committed, believing Communists, neither they nor their son was ever trusted. Another officer's elder brother had demonstrated against the invasion of Czechoslovakia in 1968 and disgraced his whole family. Melekhin, the chief engineer and Ramius' equal in rank, had never been allowed the route to command simply because his superiors wanted him to be an engineer. Borodin, who was ready for his own command, had once accused a *zampolit* of homosexuality; the man he had informed on was the son of the chief *zampolit* of the Northern Fleet. There are many paths to treason.[15]

Critics have always credited Tom Clancy with having a vivid and unerring instinct for the scientific and technical details contained in his spy novels. Indeed, many wondered in the beginning whether he did not have some unexplained access to classified defense information. He always replied that there is a wealth of open-source technical defense information in trade publications like *Aerospace Daily*. The observations quoted above, however, make it equally clear that he understands in human terms what motivated some spies to work in place or defect from the Soviet Union. The corruption of the Soviet system was a great motivator for espionage, if Western intelligence agencies could get close enough to its victims to exploit it. And for a good many years, Soviet military equipment— planes, tanks, radars: what the U.S. government bureaucratically shorthanded to SOVMAT (Soviet materiel)—was a primary collection target.

Marko Ramius's complaints about the Soviet Union find their echo in the real-world actions of Colonel Oleg Penkovsky, who is widely regarded as the most significant Western spy of the Cold War era.

The Penkovsky case offers insights into all the spy lore that has been discussed thus far: recruitment, betrayal, bureaucracy, counterintelligence, and tradecraft. Although Penkovsky did not come forward until July 1960, his determination to betray the Soviet Union and supply "illegal information" to the West was being formed as early as his service in Turkey, in 1955–1956, as deputy military attaché in the Soviet embassy. There, he met and befriended U.S. Army attaché Colonel Charles Maclean Peeke, a towering figure six feet, five inches tall, who impressed Penkovsky mightily. Nonetheless, it took Penkovsky four more years and several frustrating attempts before he could make contact with the Americans.

It seems ridiculous in retrospect that Penkovsky had to throw himself into the arms of two American student tourists on the Moskvoretsky Bridge in Moscow on a rainy August night in 1960, with several pages of incriminating Soviet defense information on his person, in order to *volunteer* his services as a spy for the West. Yet so vigorous were the counterintelligence measures of the KGB to prevent unauthorized contacts between Soviet citizens and Western businessmen in the Soviet Union that Western embassies briefed all their visitors to view volunteers making offers like Penkovsky as provocations likely to lead to their imprisonment or expulsion from the U.S.S.R. In fact, before making his successful overture to the two students, Penkovsky had been blown off by members of visiting trade delegations, and when there was no immediate response to his August 1960 bridge encounter, he tried to establish additional contact with a Canadian and later a British delegation and was rebuffed.

What is clear in the Penkovsky case and in many other successful Western spy cases during the Cold War is that foreign officials at high levels were often drawn to Western diplomats, especially Americans, who projected the confidence and sense of control that Dewey Clarridge said he had learned in Officer Candidate School at Fort Benning. Whether it was the "aura of command" that Tom Rogers displayed to haul in PECOCK in the fictional *Agents of Innocence,* or the *zakuski,* the typical Russian hors d'oeuvres that Kisevalter served Popov to ease his mind during agent meetings, the glamour of assisting the "winning" side in the struggle between Communist and capitalist ideologies helped foreign officials to commit treason. This was in marked contrast to the situation that obtained in the 1930s, when the future of capitalism during the Great Depression was not so clear. For the generation of foreigners after World War II, however, America was *where it was at,* to use the vernacular. The idea that by getting close to and helping U.S. officials one might one day have a chance to visit or even live in the United States motivated more than one spy for the West.

In John le Carré's world, it might have explained the treachery of Kim Philby, who in the person of Bill Haydon in *Tinker, Tailor* saw the spy dominion of the Englishman, schooled to empire, usurped and overwhelmed by the "ugly," moneyed American cousins, and deeply resented it.

Penkovsky of course admired Colonel Peeke, but he brought other baggage to his decision to spy for the West. He believed that the fact that his father had been an aristocrat and had fought for the White Army in the 1920s would prevent him from ever advancing to the rank of general in the GRU, the Soviet military intelligence service, even though he, Penkovsky, had had an exemplary record in the Great Patriotic War from 1941 to 1945. Penkovsky's situation was further complicated by the fact that he had merely stated to the KGB that his father had died of typhus in 1919, and it was they who had determined his real history.

Furthermore, Penkovsky had wormed his way into the upper regions of the Soviet defense establishment through his friendship with his surrogate father, General Sergei Varentsov. In addition to supplying Penkovsky with valuable spy information to pass to the West, this relationship gave him an insight into the nearly feudal relationships between high-ranking Communist Party members and their vassal protégés and underlings. Not believing he had a chance to make it to the top rung in the inner circle of the Communist Party elite, Penkovsky began to chafe at the arbitrary unfairness and hypocrisy in the privileges accorded this self-selected group.

Finally, Penkovsky was himself quite vain and venal. He liked to think of himself as an extraordinary talent whose depths had been neither plumbed nor appreciated. He paid elaborate homage to his new Western masters, seeking the recognition he had never received in the U.S.S.R. His Western case officers played to this weakness by photographing him in the uniforms of both a British and a U.S. Army colonel and delivering personal notes from the directors of British and American intelligence.

Despite these many potential complications, Penkovsky delivered the espionage goods to the West for more than two years. He was a diligent and meticulous spy, copying and photographing with his CIA-supplied Minox camera more than ten thousand pages of sensitive Soviet war plans, nuclear missile diagrams, and highly classified military information.

Furthermore, Penkovsky understood the importance of the information he was clandestinely supplying the West. He had been first in his class of eighty students in rocket school in the military and thereby obtained the right to sit in on the most advanced lectures and briefings about Soviet missilery, which knowledge he put to good use for his Western collaborators.

Penkovsky's great contribution to Western intelligence came during the Cuban Missile Crisis of October 1962, when he was able to depict for President Kennedy in detailed drawings the precise characteristics of the medium- and intermediate-range ballistic missiles Khrushchev was proposing to install in Cuba. By this time, the United States was beginning to acquire thousands of satellite and U-2 photographs showing the transportation, landing, concealment, and eventual installation of Soviet MRBMs and IRBMs on the island, and lots of SIGINT revealing the size of the Soviet military detachment, but Penkovsky's reports made clear the capabilities of the weapons and the more important fact that Khrushchev was pushing the limit of the Soviet Union's military and logistical reach with this effort. Penkovsky revealed the extent of Khrushchev's difficulties at home, the crisis among the nationalities, the absence of consumer goods in a grim domestic economy, and the fact that Khrushchev was often at odds with the Soviet military high command.

Indeed, it was Penkovsky's constant reporting that Khrushchev's bellicose rhetoric toward the West was *not* backed up by the extensive arsenal of ballistic missiles Khrushchev claimed to have that contributed to JFK's confidence in October 1962 that the emplacement of missiles on Cuba might well have been Khrushchev's gamble alone, rather than a move fully planned in advance and supported by the Politburo. Similar advice was being given President Kennedy by former ambassador to the U.S.S.R. Llewellyn Thompson. One can make a strong argument that these concurring views, Penkovsky's and

Thompson's—one covert, the other private but open—helped persuade the president that the quarantine option was the best opening gambit in getting Khrushchev to step back from the brink. In any event, it represents the perfect illustration of the importance of the human spy in the mix with all the other bits and pieces of information presidents and chiefs of state rely on to help decipher the thinking and intentions of a potential adversary. *Confirming* and *amplifying* information acquired by other means is often the role spy information plays best.

This is how one authoritative account described Penkovsky and his work product:

> Reports and Requirements separated Penkovsky's material into two categories of highly classified reports created especially for the operation. One series of reports dealt with the documents Penkovsky photographed and sent to the West. This was known as the IRONBARK series. The other category dealt with Penkovsky's subjective reporting on personalities and their comments on vital issues. This was named the CHICKADEE series. Included in this second category were Penkovsky's own impressions of political and military developments based on his sources' information.
>
> Penkovsky's dynamism and enthusiasm, his wide-ranging and passionate denunciations of the Soviet system and its leaders, illustrated with anecdotes, fascinated and captivated the American and British teams. Never before had there been a Soviet spy like him.[16]

This may have been so, but the downside of the operation was that Penkovsky was a handful. The arduous circumstances of his throwing himself at various indifferent Western repre-

OLEG PENKOVSKY
The Soviet GRU colonel who volunteered to the U.S. and U.K. intelligence services and supplied the most sensitive military and political human source intelligence to the West during the Cold War. Penkovsky's information was critical to President John F. Kennedy's understanding of Premier Nikita Khrushchev's mind-set and strategy during the Cuban Missile Crisis of October 1962. Shown here in a U.S. Army colonel's uniform in 1961.

Left: Penkovsky in a British army colonel's uniform in London, 1961.

Below: Penkovsky in dress uniform with the medals he received for his bravery during World War II.

sentatives before he finally made contact with SIS and the CIA may have been remarkably good fortune given the Soviet counterintelligence roadblocks normally arrayed against such an attempt, but they seem to have convinced Penkovsky that his mission was divinely blessed, that he was unassailable, and that he was destined to become the most productive Russian spy the West had ever encountered. He took enormous risks with the documents he "borrowed" and feverishly copied and photographed, even late in the game, when he and his handlers had reason to suspect that counterintelligence attention might be focusing on him.

Luckily, his handlers were the best the British and American intelligence services had on their rolls: Joseph Bulik and George Kisevalter (of Popov fame) got the assignment for the CIA; and Michael Stokes and Harold Shergold for MI6. Shergold had just successfully obtained a confession from longtime Soviet penetration of SIS George Blake, who among other acts of betrayal had compromised Popov and the Berlin Tunnel to the KGB. These spy runners possessed a wealth of operational know-how about the Soviet Union and how to maintain the tradecraft necessary to protect a valuable penetration agent like Penkovsky. Yet he drove them to distraction with his quirky narcissism and thirst for recognition. He was also stubborn and willful about his tradecraft, insisting on such operational obsessions as loading a favorite dead drop, behind the radiator in the entrance hall across from the pay phone in the apartment building between the meat store and the shoe store on Pushkinskaya Street in Moscow, even though it was located in a prominent neighborhood and he had used it countless times. Penkovsky was so driven to keep his Western collaborators apprised of the latest developments affecting Khrushchev's leadership of the U.S.S.R. in 1962 that he continued his regular brush-pass contacts with Janet Chisholm, the wife of a British diplomat in Moscow and his regular contact, long after it was operationally prudent to do so. There was just no slowing him down.

Perhaps the unsung hero of the Penkovsky operation, however, was a British businessman, Greville Wynne, who was neither a professional spy nor a spy runner. Wynne had led delegations of British businessmen to the Soviet Union on buying expeditions and hosted Soviet delegations in Britain in return; and he had met and could continue to meet Penkovsky in an official capacity. British SIS recruited him to serve as a courier, and Wynne was fully occupied in servicing Penkovsky's personal and operational needs from the beginning to the end of his service to the West. He was so close to Penkovsky that he was arrested as a spy in Budapest and hauled back to Moscow to stand trial at the same time the KGB arrested Penkovsky. Wynne was convicted and imprisoned, then exchanged for a Soviet spy caught in the West. Penkovsky did not fare as well. He was tried, convicted, and shot for treason in May 1963.

Could Penkovsky's Western masters have anticipated the operational security lapses that might have tipped off the KGB to his spying? It was pretty clear that the KGB suspected something toward the end, in that they refused to permit Penkovsky to travel with trade delegations that he had had no difficulty getting permission to accompany before. Wynne came under suspicion as well. Penkovsky believed he was being followed in some of his attempted brush contacts with Janet Chisolm in early 1962, and KGB surveillance photography introduced at Penkovsky's trial proved he was correct.

Nonetheless, Penkovsky appears to have been determined to see his effort through despite the entreaties of his handlers to go slow, and he was reluctant to suspend activities to reestablish operational contact and pull the rip cord activating his emergency escape plan. Perhaps it was a final burst of his belief in his own immortality.

With Penkovsky's arrest, the West lost its most productive human spy of the Cold War, even though his service had lasted barely more than two years. What he was able to convey about the then current state of the Soviet military; conditions generally in the U.S.S.R.; and the state of play between Khrushchev and the senior members of his Politburo was unique information at the time and without question helped President Kennedy better manage the twin crises of Berlin in 1961 and Cuba in 1962.

A final echo of the fictional Marko Ramius's decision to make the Soviet state pay for its crimes against the Russian people is the TRIGON case. "TRIGON" was the cryptonym assigned to Aleksandr Dmitrievich Ogorodnik. He was a Soviet diplomat who volunteered to spy for U.S. intelligence in Bogotá, Colombia, in the mid-1980s. TRIGON's family had been decimated by the Stalinist purges in the late 1930s, and he was determined to gain revenge. He brought his CIA case officer all the sensitive information that crossed his desk in Colombia, and then announced one day that he was being transferred home to Moscow, where he was slated to serve in the operations center of the Soviet Foreign Ministry. There he would see all the foreign diplomatic communications traffic worldwide, going and coming.

TRIGON was a highly productive spy for the United States in Moscow for several more years, until he came to his case officer, Jack Downing, one day and asked for "the pill." Downing, who was the CIA chief in Moscow at the time (and a superb American intelligence officer who later became the deputy director for operations at the CIA, and thus America's top spy runner), replied that he had no authority to supply TRIGON with a suicide pill. It was not the way the CIA did business. TRIGON responded by saying that if the United States wanted him to continue to bring out Soviet secrets from the Foreign Ministry, it would have to supply him with "the pill." TRIGON knew the KGB's track record at catching Western spies, and he was aware of what they did when they caught one. He figured the KGB would get him sooner or later, and he did not wish to be interrogated and tortured.

Downing deliberated the matter for a time and discussed it with CIA Headquarters. There was really no question that TRIGON was right. Western spies had been successfully exfiltrated before capture on several occasions, but a number had been caught without warning, like Popov and Penkovsky, and executed. This was a tough call for Downing and for the CIA. Indeed, in handling TRIGON, Downing was regularly exposing himself and his family to danger from the KGB by using them as cover, when they would cross-country ski as a family in Moscow city parks on a Sunday while Jack unloaded a TRIGON dead drop. There was a lot at stake in the TRIGON operation.

In the end, TRIGON was given his suicide pill, a cyanide capsule fitted as the top of an ordinary ballpoint pen, and, as he had foreseen, there came a time when the KGB did catch up to him. He didn't hesitate for a second. He snatched his ballpoint, presumably to sign his confession, bit off the cyanide capsule, and was gone. Witnesses observed that he was dead before he hit the floor.

Seven

Spies and Sex

When Tatiana Romanova is recruited by Soviet intelligence to seduce James Bond and deliver him to an assassin in Ian Fleming's *From Russia, With Love,* it is not a consensual matter. Her superior, the repugnant Rosa Klebb, herself an aggressive lesbian, puts the question to Tatiana as follows:

> "For the next few weeks you will be most carefully trained for this operation until you know exactly what to do in all contingencies. You will be taught certain foreign customs. You will be equipped with beautiful clothes. You will be instructed in all the arts of allurement. Then you will be sent to a foreign country, somewhere in Europe. There you will meet this man. You will seduce him. In this matter you will have no silly compunctions. Your body belongs to the State. Since your birth, the State has nourished it. Now your body must work for the State. Is that understood?"
>
> "Yes, Comrade Colonel." The logic was inescapable.[1]

Since Delilah seduced Samson to rob him of his strength, it has been assumed that the full panoply of feminine wiles is available to serve a political master, in battle or in espionage, when the fate of a tribe or nation is at stake. And spy literature has also depended on this assumption. Recall how Liz Gold worms her way into Alec Leamas's bed in *The Spy Who Came In from the Cold* to become the recipient of Control's largesse, thereby unwittingly undercutting Leamas's testimony that Mundt is an SIS spy. The fact that she did not know the role which she was being called upon to play does not detract from its effectiveness.

Sex also operates successfully to affect the outcome of a spy operation in the literature, even when it is quite incidental to the recruitment of a spy. Remember Maurice Castle's gratitude to Carson and through him the Communist Party and the U.S.S.R., when Carson exfiltrates Sarah and Sam from South Africa, moments ahead of the pursuing South African Bureau of State Security (BOSS) in *The Human Factor.* Castle had fallen in love with Sarah independent of any Communist or espionage direction, but the Soviets reaped the reward of their South African brethren's assistance to her at a moment of great danger.

In spy operations where sex plays a part, the initiative does not always come from the female. Witness Bill Haydon's seduction of George Smiley's weak, fashionable, and unfaithful wife Ann in *Tinker, Tailor.* Smiley unravels the mystery of why at the moment of Haydon's unmasking. It was at the direction of Karla, Smiley's Soviet archnemesis:

> Before he left, Smiley asked the one question he still cared about.
>
> "I'll have to break it to Ann. Is there anything particular you want me to pass on to her?"
>
> It was Karla's idea, he [Haydon] explained. Karla had long recognized that Smiley represented the

biggest threat to the mole Gerald. "He said you were quite good."

"Thank you."

"But you had this one price: Ann. The last illusion of the illusionless man. He reckoned that if I were known to be Ann's lover around the place you wouldn't see me very straight when it came to other things." His eyes, Smiley noticed, had become very fixed. Pewtery, Ann called them. "Not to strain it or anything but, if it was possible, join the queue. Point?"

"Point," said Smiley."[2]

This, of course, finds echoes in the real world. According to press reports, one of the methods used by the French intelligence service in 1994 to break the alleged American economic espionage effort against French technology was to seduce a female American spy who was operating in Paris under private business cover. Reportedly, she involved her Swiss-Brazilian lover in efforts to cultivate well-placed French officials, but all the time, he was reporting her contacts to French intelligence.

Incidental sex has been a factor in the real world of espionage since long before the escapades of Mata Hari. What is of greater interest to us, however, is sex used as an offensive weapon, a tool in espionage operations, utilized as part of the technique of cultivation and recruitment of spies, as well as their entrapment. As described ideally by Fleming in *From Russia, With Love*, Soviet intelligence had long incorporated the practice of setting sexual "honey traps" in its approaches to potential European and American sources from the earliest days of the Soviet emergence into the international community in the 1930s. The Soviet intelligence services would send "swallows" to seduce Western businessmen in their hotel

rooms in Moscow, or Allied servicemen and Occupation officials in Berlin or Vienna after World War II. Recordings were
made of the sexual liaisons, and photographs or films taken by
Soviet intelligence operatives, and the Westerner was confronted with the choice of either cooperating with the KGB or
being exposed. It worked so well for the Soviets that the first
CIA intelligence chief in Moscow in the late 1950s was compromised, along with a number of his officers and fellow
embassy officials. As a result, when the victims told Ambassador Charles Bohlen what had taken place, the ambassador,
who had not theretofore been informed of the presence of a
CIA officer on his staff, petitioned President Eisenhower to
have them all recalled to the United States.

What made this technique of sexual entrapment so successful for the Soviets, however, was not easily reproduced by
Western intelligence services operating in Europe, Asia, or the
United States. In the period after World War II, Berlin under
Four Powers occupation, Vienna, and Moscow were such hostile environments, which Soviet intelligence could control so
completely, that approaches from attractive females to lonely,
pressured Westerners who should have known better were
remarkably successful. Aside from the fact that few Western
intelligence services could dictate to their nationals that their
bodies belonged to the State à la Tatiana Romanova, the circumstances of approach, cultivation, and recruitment/entrap-
ment of potential intelligence sources were much different in
the West. The human targets were not so isolated, not so far
from other forms of sexual delinquency, or from help in the
event they were compromised, that the technique of sexual
entrapment would work as well.

Also, it would appear that the straitlaced morality of the Vic-
torian era had not entirely disappeared from the thinking of
many Westerners who were caught up in Soviet-contrived sexual dalliances. These Westerners responded to threats of black-

mail as if they were traveling salesmen caught out on a bender, rather than worldly diplomats or professionals for whom the threat of exposure might be managed satisfactorily. By contrast, Soviet targets of sexual entrapment operations would invariably laugh off the threat of exposure as not very compelling in their culture.

In any event, for whatever reasons—scruples, bureaucratic clumsiness, or the lack of a cooperative "swallow" population— the British, French, and American intelligence services made less use of sexual entrapment operations in the decades after World War II than did the Soviets.

It should be noted that the sex employed in espionage operations was not all heterosexual. Miranda Carter's recent book on Anthony Blunt hints at the role homosexual liaisons might have played in his own recruitment, and his recruitment of others, to the Communist cause at Cambridge in the 1930s. But it does not pretend to identify Blunt's homosexuality and the prevalence of it in his effete circle of friends as a primary factor. Homosexuality was just a part of the scene—for some, apparently, even a rite of passage. It is likely, however, that the intimacy achieved in homosexual unions with other impressionable Cambridge undergraduates of that era created opportunities for Blunt and Guy Burgess, another member of the notorious Cambridge Five, to make the case easier for recruitment to the Communist banner.

More recently, it has been surmised that State Department economic officer Felix Bloch's ravenous and expensive appetite for heterosexual sadomasochistic sex while serving in Vienna in 1981 spawned a need for cash to help him satisfy his bizarre sexual cravings, and thus delivered him into the hands of Soviet intelligence. Bloch was never caught and prosecuted, probably because FBI spy Robert P. Hanssen tipped off the Soviets to the FBI's investigation of him. But according to David Wise's vivid account of Hanssen's treachery, it seems pretty clear that

Bloch's sexual habits created the vulnerability that the Soviets then exploited for espionage purposes.[3]

The saddest case of sexual exploitation of an American for spying purposes during the Cold War, however, is that of Marine Corps Sergeant Clayton J. Lonetree. Lonetree, a Native American from Minnesota who was the product of a broken home, enlisted in the Marine Corps while he was still in high school in January 1980. Two months after graduating from high school, he went on active duty; after boot camp and infantry training, he spent his first tour of duty at Guantánamo Bay, Cuba, where he stayed a year.

After a stint in an orphanage with his younger brother and sister, Lonetree had been raised in St. Paul by a proud, demanding father who pushed him to achieve beyond his level of capability. Seemingly an ideal candidate for noncommissioned officer rank in the Marines, Lonetree followed orders with tenacity and complete obedience. His limitations were equally clear. He was not very bright, and the loneliness and emptiness of his upbringing had left him with a low sense of self-worth and a profound feeling of insecurity. He read a number of trashy spy novels and fantasized a lot about exploits of derring-do. He also apparently formed a positive fixation on Adolf Hitler with which he importuned girlfriends, acquaintances, and anybody else willing to listen. Finally, and understandably because of his youth and very limited travel and life experience, he appears to have been quite naïve and gullible.

This created a perfect recipe for disaster in the next assignment for which Lonetree applied, in August 1984: the Marines' elite embassy-guard school in Quantico, Virginia. Turned down at first, Lonetree was later accepted after one of Minnesota's U.S. senators exerted pressure on his behalf. After completing his guard training, Lonetree was assigned to the U.S. embassy in Moscow. For an individual of Lonetree's cast of mind, the posting could not have been less appropriate. It was cold and lonely all of the time in the Moscow embassy, with factors of economic class and education separating the guards from other Foreign Service personnel, few single women around in the embassy, substandard barracks for the Marine guards at that time, and a strict limitation on the guards' personal privileges and mobility in the city itself. Also, an inexplicably lax attitude seems to have been demanded of the guards in examining the credentials of embassy personnel as they entered or exited the chancery. Apparently the embassy staff expected to be physically recognized by the guards without presenting formal identification documents, and this appears to have undercut the strict application of security procedures in one of the most challenging diplomatic posts in the world. This casual attitude apparently carried over to fraternization with local women, despite the strict prohibition against it. Against all the rules, some Marines were dating Soviet women at the time.

In addition, Lonetree's longtime girlfriend and fellow Marine stateside wrote him to announce that she had married another Marine. Lonetree's loneliness was by all accounts acute and intensifying.

Into this dismal picture walked an embassy interpreter, a Ukrainian Jew named Violetta Sanni, and Lonetree fell for her, hook, line, and sinker. Violetta was single, living with her divorced mother and sister. Lonetree began to accompany Violetta home from the embassy until she warned him that she might lose her job if the KGB found out. He then began to employ countersurveillance routes and techniques that he had gleaned from his spy novels to accompany her. In November 1985, Lonetree apparently took Violetta to the Marine Corps Ball, the biggest social event of the year for the Marine detachment. Nobody appeared to object or called him to account.

From this point, matters went steadily downhill, not quickly but irreversibly. Violetta and Lonetree became lovers. She introduced him to "Uncle Sasha," who began to ask him questions, innocent at first but focusing in time on the location of certain offices in the embassy, and the names of selected personnel, in typical KGB fashion. Finally, in one of their later meetings, Uncle Sasha pulled a list of intelligence requirements from his pocket and it became clear to Lonetree that he was dealing with the KGB. He did not report the contacts with Sasha or his relationship with Violetta to his superiors, he later confessed, for fear of the consequences to her. It also appears that he liked the cloak-and-dagger aspect of the relationship. It pushed him into the fantasy world of his spy novels, and he felt he could safely judge when the questions were drawing him into forbidden security territory.

In March 1986, Lonetree finished his tour in Moscow, and at his request was transferred to the U.S. embassy in Vienna, the spy capital of the world. Uncle Sasha followed him to Vienna, bringing a love letter and photos from Violetta, and gradually began to levy requirements on Lonetree for intelligence information about the Vienna embassy. It was in steady progression that Lonetree delivered what he described as a recently discarded embassy telephone book to Sasha, and then floor plans of the chancery, both for a total of $3,600 in cash and a secret visit to Violetta in Moscow. By this time, Lonetree knew he was in way over his head. After Uncle Sasha introduced him to a high-ranking Vienna-based KGB "handler" who began to discuss future spy training with him, Lonetree turned himself in to the chief CIA representative in Vienna on December 14, 1986.

Lonetree was turned over to the Naval Investigative Service in late December 1986; returned to the United States and charged with espionage in January 1987; court-martialed and found guilty in August 1987; and sentenced to thirty years in prison. His sentence was later reduced to fifteen years, and he was eventually released in 1996, having served eight. There had been great confusion at the time of his arrest as to the extent of the security compromises Lonetree had permitted at both embassies, but in fact, though egregious enough, they had not entailed Soviet intelligence officers wandering freely in the classified areas of the chancery building in Moscow, as originally had been thought.

Clayton Lonetree has never acknowledged that Violetta Sanni was a spy. He believed that her vulnerability as a Jew and embassy employee caused her to turn him over to Uncle Sasha and the KGB. Seasoned intelligence observers have concluded, however, that Violetta's behavior was a virtuoso KGB "swallow" performance that worked to a charm against a guileless, lonely, insecure Marine guard who probably should never have been selected for this line of work, and surely should never have found himself assigned to Moscow or Vienna.

Recognizing that sex incidental to espionage is as much a part of the equation as alcohol abuse or the other properties of a life of great strain and deception, the question is, does it work as a practical tool for spy recruitment? The answer appears to be that it worked better in the Soviet spy culture directed against the West during the Cold War than it did or does for Western intelligence services against Soviet and other targets. As noted previously, some part of this may have more to do with the cold, lonely, and controlled circumstances under which the Soviets most often applied the "honey trap" technique than with the disparate cultural vulnerabilities of the two sides during the Cold War, but sexual entrapment appears to occupy a less favored place in the arsenal of the Western intelligence services. Another part may have to do with a preference for positive reinforcement as a technique of spy recruitment over coercion and intimidation. It may be that

Dewey Clarridge's "follow me" approach or Tom Rogers's effort to get a spy to want to do what you need to have done works better over the long haul than instilling the fear of being exposed as unfaithful or a sexual deviant. In any case, sex and spies will always be part of the espionage equation.

Eight

Assassination

Political assassination is a dirty business, whether it be a mission assigned to the intelligence services or one assigned to a military authority. Historically, the intelligence services have recoiled from it, largely because the competencies required to pull it off are quite different from those required in classical espionage. And spies don't like involving themselves in planning and carrying out political assassinations. It's not what they were hired to do. Somerset Maugham states the old-fashioned objection succinctly, in *Ashenden:*

> It was not of course a thing that the big-wigs cared to have anything to do with. Though ready enough to profit by the activities of obscure agents of whom they had never heard, they shut their eyes to dirty work so that they could put their clean hands on their hearts and congratulate themselves that they had never done anything that was unbecoming to men of honour. Ashenden thought with cynical humour of an incident in his relations with R. He had been approached with an offer that he thought it his duty to put before his chief.
>
> "By the way," he said to him as casually as possi-

ble, "I've got a sportsman who's willing to assassinate King B. for five thousand pounds."

King B. was the ruler of a Balkan state which was on the verge through his influence of declaring war against the Allies and it was evident that his disappearance from the scene would be extremely useful. His successor's sympathies were indefinite and it might be possible to persuade him to keep his country neutral. Ashenden saw from R.'s quick, intent look that he was perfectly aware of the situation. But he frowned sulkily.

"Well, what of it?"

"I told him I'd transmit his offer. I believe he's perfectly genuine. He's pro-Ally and he thinks it would bust his country if it went on the side of the Germans."

"What's he want five thousand pounds for, then?"

"It's a risk and if he does the Allies a good turn he doesn't see why he shouldn't get something out of it."

R. shook his head energetically.

"It's not the kind of thing we can have anything to do with. We don't wage war by those methods. We leave them to the Germans. Damn it all, we are gentlemen."[1]

Present-day objections would not be put in the language of the gentleman's code (so strongly reminiscent of U.S. Secretary of State Henry L. Stimson's oft-quoted statement in 1929, as he closed down his department's fledgling but highly successful SIGINT operations, that "gentlemen don't read other gentlemen's mail"). But the result is the same. Current intelligence community leadership would echo the response that political assassinations are not what spy agencies should be about.

The pitfalls are further demonstrated in spy fiction, by, for example, the Jackal's straight talk to his potential Organization for a French Algeria employers as they interview him, a professional assassin, for the assignment of shooting President Charles de Gaulle of France, in Frederick Forsyth's *The Day of the Jackal.* The Jackal makes it perfectly clear that the earlier attempts on de Gaulle's life by amateur assassins drawn from the ranks of the OAS have roiled the waters for his assignment:

> "There is no man in the world who is proof against an assassin's bullet," said the Englishman. "DeGaulle's exposure rate is very high. Of course, it's possible to kill him. The point is that the chances of escape would not be too high. A fanatic prepared to die himself in the attempt is always the most certain method of eliminating a dictator who exposes himself to the public. . . ."

There follows Forsyth's discussion of the attributes of a professional assassin, quoted earlier: detachment, ruthlessness, and an ability to plan his escape. Then the Jackal is asked the sixty-four-thousand-dollar question: whether in fact a professional could kill President de Gaulle and escape.

> "In principle, yes," he replied at length. "In principle, it is always possible with enough time and planning. But in this case it would be extremely difficult. More so than with most other targets."
>
> "Why more than others?" asked Montclair.
>
> "Because DeGaulle is forewarned—not about the specific attempts but about the general intention. All big men have bodyguards and security men, but over a period of years without any serious attempt on the life of the big man, the checks

become formal, the routines mechanical, and the degree of watchfulness is lowered. The single bullet that finishes the target is wholly unexpected and therefore provokes panic. Under cover of this the assassin escapes. In this case there will be no lowering of the level of watchfulness, no mechanical routines, and if the bullet were to get to the target, there would be many who would not panic but would go for the assassin. It could be done, but it would be one of the hardest jobs in the world at this moment. You see, gentlemen, your own efforts have not only failed but have queered the pitch for everyone else."[2]

This is highly relevant to the dilemma confronting the U.S. and British governments and intelligence services in 2003, as they might have contemplated an operation to assassinate President Saddam Hussein of Iraq. Earlier failed covert action attempts to remove him from power may have destroyed the possibilities, even for a professional assassin. Today, editorialists continue to write that the new Bush doctrine of preemption argues for a resuscitation of the possibility of political assassination to prevent an unpredictable enemy from gaining weapons of mass destruction that would be used against it, "but it is unlikely to be a task given to the intelligence services. They don't want it."[3]

Spy novelist Charles McCarry wrote a book, *The Tears of Autumn*, about two notorious and successful political assassinations in 1963, which were linked in his telling of the story. McCarry's protagonist, Paul Christopher, a senior CIA clandestine operative, develops the theory that President John F. Kennedy's assassination was carried out by a gunman, Lee Harvey Oswald, who had been hired through Cuban intermediaries by the Vietnamese Ngo family to avenge the earlier

slayings of Ngo Dinh Diem and Ngo Dinh Nhu at the direction
of the U.S. government.[4] Here is how the surviving head of the
Ngo family, the Truong toc, reacts to Christopher's theory:

"Mr. Christopher," said the Truong toc, speaking the
name for the first time, "I'm curious—how did you
come to hear the name Le Thu?"

"Nguyen Kim mentioned it. He seemed to think
it would be a great joke to use it as an introduction to
you."

"And you thought it had great significance—that
it symbolized this assassination you think we carried
out?"

"I didn't know," Christopher said. "That was one
of my questions."

"You've translated the name, I understand. It
means 'the tears of autumn.' "

"Yes—if it's a code name it's poetic, but it's insecure."

"And you wish to know the name of our relative in
the North Vietnamese intelligence service?"

"Yes."

"That is all you require to prove our guilt, and rid
our country of the Americans, who, as you suggest,
will destroy it for reasons of their own policy?"

"Yes."

As Christopher and the Truong toc spoke to each
other, they smiled—more broadly with each question and answer. After hearing Christopher's final
reply, the Truong toc laughed, a string of dry barks
like the cough of a man who has swallowed smoke.
His laughter was a compliment. Only a clandestine
mind like Christopher's, free from values and concerned with nothing but the results of action, could

have conceived the proposal Christopher had just made. The Truong toc had the same sort of mind. He was delighted to encounter another brain so like his own.

"We've heard a good deal about you since yesterday, Mr. Christopher," he said. "It all seems to be true. This really is a most clever provocation. I have no idea what purpose your masters think it will serve, but you may give them my answer. It is this: your hypothesis is absurd. How could we touch a Kennedy? They live in another dimension of power."[5]

Ronald Goldfarb has examined the real-life counterpart to the McCarry novel. In *Perfect Villains, Imperfect Heroes*, Goldfarb explores the allegation that the Mob, in the persons of Messrs. Sam Giancana, Santos Trafficante, Jr., and John Rosselli, together with the Teamsters' Jimmy Hoffa, conspired to assassinate first Bobby Kennedy and then JFK for double-crossing them by pursuing an all-out war against organized crime and racketeering, even as the CIA was enlisting Giancana and Rosselli in the effort to assassinate Fidel Castro on the Kennedys' behalf.[6] Goldfarb observes that although there is no proof of the Mob's having hired Oswald to commit the act, the statements of Trafficante, Giancana, and others that they would get JFK might well be admissible in court in a conspiracy prosecution, presumably as declarations against interest, demonstrating a motive for the assassination. It's the coincidental involvement of the CIA in plotting the assassination of Castro with help from Giancana and Rosselli that makes this relevant to our deliberations. It created the "quid" that at least some of the gangsters believed should have yielded the "quo" of the Kennedy brothers' laying off the Mob. Since it didn't, it produced an articulated reaction of betrayal and a cry for revenge.

Did President Kennedy know about the CIA's plan to use the Mob to assassinate Castro? Probably, although there is no written record. The first contacts between the Agency's Sheffield Edwards and Sam Giancana apparently took place in the latter days of the Eisenhower administration. President Kennedy may have been brought into the picture when DCI Allen Dulles and Richard Bissell, his director of operations (then euphemistically called "plans"), briefed him on the Bay of Pigs operation in November 1960, after the election, in Palm Beach. Bobby Kennedy probably learned about it some months later. In any event, from the records of the Church Committee investigating the allegations of CIA abuses in 1975–1976, it is clear that Bobby Kennedy knew about the CIA's clandestine efforts to eliminate Fidel Castro, including the use of Giancana and Rosselli, by the spring of 1962, when he was directing Operation Mongoose, which had the same mission, on the president's behalf. When all is said and done, however, even though there might have been ample grounds for the Mob to believe that the Kennedys were unfairly out to get them, given all that they had attempted to do for the CIA and the U.S. government, the two principal bodies that studied the Kennedy assassination, the Warren Commission and the House Committee on Assassinations, found no evidence that either the Mob or Castro had hired Oswald to kill the President.

McCarry's fictional portrait of the Ngo family plot to assassinate JFK and Goldfarb's musings about the Mob's wannabe role illustrate what might take place if the intelligence services of one nation systematically decided to eliminate the leader of another. This is one of the real-world reasons why the CIA and the British SIS now doesn't assassinate rival heads of state, or intelligence officers either, for that matter. Once one starts down that road, there is no end to the possibilities of tit-for-tat killings. It's a mug's game.

The Israelis have targeted and assassinated Palestinian intelligence officials on many occasions since 1948, and their experience appears to bear out the following proposition: If you target the opposition security service, it will target you in response; then killing just begets killing. It is endless.

In the U.S., there was a time during the Cold War when the CIA was directed to plot and carry out the assassination of foreign government leaders: Lumumba, Julián Trujillo, Castro, and Allende to name a few. When the circumstances and details of the assassination plots were uncovered by the U.S. Senate investigation of allegations of CIA wrongdoing, carried out under the direction of Senator Frank Church in 1975–1976, the result was an executive order promulgated by President Ford prohibiting CIA involvement, direct or indirect, in political assassinations. In fact, none of the assassination plots mounted by the CIA before the ban was ever successfully carried out, but it was not for want of trying on the part of the Agency. Since the Ford executive order in 1976, the prohibition on assassination by the CIA has been retained in the successive executive orders on intelligence promulgated by Presidents Carter and Reagan. By and large, at the turn of the twenty-first century, the settled opinion seems to have been that the downside risks of involving U.S. intelligence in targeted political assassinations outweighed the benefits. Simply put, the questions of accountability, suitability, and appropriateness had introduced complications that went beyond the issue of what might be gained by eliminating a noxious foreign leader. As former DCI Richard Helms once observed, how can you be sure if you eliminate leader X that he won't be replaced by someone even worse?

In President George W. Bush's current war on terrorism, however, the fabric of the ban on political assassinations seems to be tearing a bit. The possibility of targeting suspected Al Qaeda leaders from afar and following their movements by unmanned drone aircraft like the Predator, until they are positioned for the kill, has given rise to the question of whether the president has not in fact suspended the ban on assassinations for the duration of this war. Perhaps the existence of a loose confederation of nonstate terrorists sworn to attack the West, and the United States in particular, without warning and without provocation has changed the rule on assassinations.

Finally, what is the duty owed by spy services to their own officers and countrymen? Does the ban on assassination operate here as well? Despite Graham Greene's fertile imagination in *The Human Factor,* when Dr. Percival poisons fellow spy runner Davis to eliminate a leak in the African section of MI6; or le Carré's equally bizarre approach to the failed escapes of Alec Leamas and Liz Gold in *The Spy Who Came In from the Cold;* or the execution of the mole Gerald—Bill Haydon—by his oldest friend, Jim Prideaux, in le Carré's *Tinker, Tailor,* assassination is emphatically not on among the Western intelligence services in handling problems with their own countrymen. That way madness would lie.

A similar conclusion, however, cannot as easily be reached with respect to the Soviets. In the world of fiction, Andre Szara, the hero of Alan Furst's *Dark Star,* witnesses the execution of his KGB mentor and protector Abramov, ostensibly for stealing a payoff to a nonexistent agent, but in reality for his knowledge of Stalin's clandestine overtures to Hitler prior to the signing of the Stalin-Ribbentrop Pact in 1939.[7] As Furst accurately portrays the divisions in Soviet intelligence, the Caucasus faction of conspiratorial spymasters led by Lavrenty Beria and loyal to Stalin was in constant internecine struggle with the old-line Bolshevik element, largely Jewish, that dated its service to the revolution to 1917. Stalin ruthlessly purged the Soviet intelligence services after 1938 in the same manner that he decimated the Soviet officer corps in the military, and for the same reasons: his own paranoia and a demand for absolute control.

The tradition of executions of "enemies of the state" carried out by Soviet intelligence extended to political émigrés from the Soviet Union—Leon Trotsky in Mexico City and Stefan Bandera in Western Europe—and continued into the 1950s. But it was a game reserved to Soviet intelligence. Western intelligence services did not follow the Soviet example.

Nine

Villains and Fabricators

Captain Van Donck was a brutal and simple man who believed in something, however repugnant—he was one of those one could forgive. What Castle could never bring himself to forgive was this smooth educated officer of BOSS [South African Bureau of State Security chief Cornelius Muller]. It was men of this kind—men with the education to know what they were about—that made a hell in heaven's despite. He thought of what his Communist friend Carson had so often said to him—"Our worst enemies here are not the ignorant and the simple, however cruel, our worst enemies are the intelligent and the corrupt." . . .

Castle watched him adapting, as naturally as a chameleon, to the color of the soil. . . . Perhaps he would have found Muller more likable if he had been less adaptable. All through dinner Muller made his courteous conversation. Yes, thought Castle, I really would have preferred Captain Van Donck. . . . A prejudice had something in common with an ideal. Cornelius Muller was without prejudice and he was without an ideal.[1]

It takes all kinds to make the perfect fictional villain. In *The Human Factor,* these ruminations of Soviet spy Maurice Castle about the South African intelligence official who once harassed him and sought to imprison his black agent, now wife, Sarah, are an ironic introduction to Castle's current assignment, which is to work with Muller and the Americans on Project Uncle Remus. The project is designed to give the apartheid government of South Africa nuclear means to prevent a black African revolt. In Greene's eyes this is ample justification for Castle's decision to risk all in one final act of betrayal of British intelligence.

Spy villains in the early novels of espionage are fairly obvious: they are simply the bad guys. In Kipling's *Kim,* they are the Russian and French emissaries who fall on Kim's lama (holy man) and try to beat him, until Kim intervenes and drives them away, stealing their maps and instructions into the bargain. Dollmann in Childers's *The Riddle of the Sands* is less orthodox: an Englishman and naval officer who has defected to Germany to bring his specialized knowledge of the British coast to further the Kaiser's aspirations for a blue-water navy which can defeat Britain. Verloc in Conrad's *The Secret Agent* is an inarticulate lout who seizes upon a "blood-stained inanity of so fatuous a kind" in his attempt to "produce an outrage" by blowing up the Greenwich Observatory. In Ambler's *A Coffin for Dimitrios,* Dimitrios Makropoulos is a murderer and spy for hire, who advances from the Balkan outback to the fringes of Parisian society in a career of common betrayal and criminality.

The successors to these obvious bad guys appear in Ian Fleming's *Dr. No* and *Goldfinger,* where the formula is updated slightly to introduce the frustrations of an abused half-caste or a thwarted megalomaniac.

Chacal in Forsyth's *The Day of the Jackal* is simply a cold-blooded professional assassin, loyal only to his tradecraft and the people who are paying him:

"A professional does not act out of fervour and is therefore more calm and less likely to make elementary errors. Not being idealistic, he is not likely to have second thoughts at the last minute about who else might get hurt in the explosion, or whatever method, and being a professional he has calculated the risks to the last contingency. So his chances of success on schedule are surer than anyone else, but he will not even enter into operation until he has devised a plan that will enable him not only to complete the mission, but to escape unharmed."[2]

To which one of his OAS interlocutors and future employers responds:

"I don't like that man. . . . He works alone, without allies. Such men are dangerous. One cannot control them."[3]

It is only when one gets to the spy novels of the Cold War that we begin to see a more subtle shading in the identification of good guys versus bad guys in spy villainy. The treachery is less traditional, and the evil emanates from unsuspected quarters. There are the double agents like Bill Haydon in le Carré's *Tinker, Tailor* and Magnus Pym in his *A Perfect Spy,* whose loyalty to king and country is twisted, and who have sold out their birthright. They are pretty standard villains.

There are the corrupt foreign chiefs of service: Mundt in le Carré's *The Spy Who Came In from the Cold* and Muller in Greene's *The Human Factor,* who are loathsome creatures but are working, at least temporarily, for the Western side. In fact, one is almost tempted to like Muller at times, as, faced with the necessity of working with his onetime intelligence target Castle, he lamely tries to make amends for his earlier efforts to pursue and persecute. One is being asked to overlook their essential viciousness and focus on their current attachment to the proper cause.

There are the unscrupulous bureaucrats like Control in *The Spy Who Came In from the Cold,* Hargreaves and Percival in *The Human Factor,* and the DCI in Ignatius's *Agents of Innocence* who are willing to kill, or allow to be killed, their own subordinates or agents, when it is a question of bureaucratic survival.

By comparison, the real world of spy villainy may be more pedestrian. From the West's perspective, the archvillains of the Cold War era have to be Kim Philby and his Cambridge colleagues. What Philby and the others gave to the Soviets, pound for pound, did more damage to the British and American intelligence services than any other spy or collection of spies: U.S. atomic bomb secrets, Operation Rollback details, countless names of people working on operations designed to contain Stalin and roll back the Soviet Union after World War II. If we believe his autobiography, Philby had always been a dedicated Communist and Soviet agent, from his earliest days in SIS. And that was the view of his Cambridge colleague Anthony Blunt.

However, one is tempted to regard much of Philby's testimony in *My Silent War* as disinformation at worst, disingenuous twaddle at best. It seems more likely that le Carré got it right in *Tinker, Tailor* with Bill Haydon. The strain of giving over such transcendant power and influence to the great, unwashed American masses was too much for some of Philby's generation of elite Britishers to bear. As Victor Maskell (modeled on Anthony Blunt) responded to an interviewer's question as to why he had betrayed Britain, in John Banville's *The Untouchable:* "Cowboys and Indians, my dear; cowboys and

KIM PHILBY
*The most notorious Soviet spy
in British intelligence during
the Cold War, who served as a
model for le Carré's mole in*
Tinker, Tailor, Soldier, Spy.

Indians," which, translated roughly, meant fear of boredom; but he added, "And hatred of America, of course!"[4]

America's real-life spy villains were motivated by filthy lucre more than the ideological pull of Communism, once one moved past the era of the Rosenbergs, Hiss, and Whittaker Chambers in the early 1940s. William Kampiles, who sold the technical specifications of the KH-11 spy satellite to the Soviets, and the Walker family, who betrayed the United States' nuclear ballistic submarine radar systems, did it for money and power, as if they were selling stolen jewelry to a fence. There appear to have been few ideological dimensions or pretensions to these sales.

With the appearance on the scene of Edward Lee Howard, Aldrich Ames, and more recently Robert P. Hanssen, the motivational complexion changes. Howard was a disgruntled CIA employee of the 1980s who took sophisticated knowledge of Agency operations in Moscow to the Soviets in revenge for having been summarily discharged for concealing an unsuitable lifestyle of drug use and petty crime on his preassignment polygraph examination. Once again, it seems that ideology was not a major factor in Howard's motivation to sell out, and the major embarrassment of the case lies in the United States' inability to keep Howard under surveillance after it had been determined that he had committed espionage. (Howard was reported to have died in Russia in July 2002, after having allegedly fallen while walking and striking his head on a rock.)

Aldrich Ames is the Philby of the modern era. The damage which his treachery caused to Western spying is not told merely in the numbers of spies he betrayed who were later shot, in the names and details of CIA and FBI operatives and operations against the U.S.S.R. which he gave away, or in the exposure of the CIA's counterintelligence weakness and bureaucratic ineptitude revealed by the nine-year "mole hunt" mounted to track him down. Ames's real damage to American intelligence is in his destruction of the Agency's self-respect, its sense of its own competence. Ames severely damaged the CIA's sense of self-worth, its esprit de corps—Cyrano de Bergerac's white plume—which, like all intangibles, when lost is harder to replace than bricks and mortar. As the details of the extent and manner of Ames's betrayal became public, cognoscenti in the executive and legislative branches of the U.S. government were scratching their heads and asking, like Casey Stengel, "Can't anybody play this game?" The CIA's mystique of ubiquitous omniscience, which any experienced U.S. spy runner will tell you is worth thirty points up on your batting average, was severely damaged in the eyes of the American people and the Agency's professional colleagues. For these reasons not entirely of his making, Aldrich Ames is the archvillain of the contemporary period.

Robert P. Hanssen's treachery has had a similar traumatic effect on the FBI's reputation in the counterintelligence world.

A particular form of spy villainy is fabrication. Many readers of spy fiction are familiar with the vacuum cleaner salesman Mr. Wermold in Graham Greene's *Our Man in Havana,* who supplies his spy superiors in London with drawings of Soviet missile installations in Cuba that look not unlike vacuum cleaner parts. Fabrication consists of the intentional dissemination of spy information as true, when in fact the information has been made up. It is false and does not come from the clandestine sources claimed for it.

> "His stuff was all so flashy, somehow," he was saying, undeterred. "Always looked good on the plate, but when you came to chew it over, nothing really there. That's how it seemed to me." He gave a puzzled giggle. "Same as trying to eat a pike. All bones. You'd get a report in, look it over. I say, that's jolly good, you'd think. But when you took a closer look it was boring. Yes, that's true because we already know it. . . . Yes, that's possible but we can't verify it because we've nothing on that region."[5]

This is how the eccentric British spy runner who followed Magnus Pym as the intelligence officer in charge of the bogus Greensleeves operation describes the case in le Carré's *A Perfect Spy.* And he is of course correct. Pym's Czech control and friend Axel had devised Greensleeves as a cover for Pym's meetings with him, while Pym was turning over the real thing to Czech intelligence.

Good fabricators can run their scam for a long time. In *Ashenden,* Somerset Maugham introduces us to Gustav, who was the top-paid and top-producing British spy in Germany for a year, until it was discovered that he had never left the city of Basel, Switzerland, but had made up his reports from overheard barroom chatter and gotten them posted to his wife from

German cities in an elaborate phony communications scheme. When confronted by Ashenden about his dishonesty, Gustav replies:

> "Did you think I was such a fool as to risk my life for fifty pounds a month? I love my wife. . . .
>
> "I had the chance of earning money without any difficulty. My firm stopped sending me into Germany at the beginning of the war, but I learned what I could from the other travelers, I kept my ears open in restaurants and beer-cellars, and I read the German papers. I got a lot of amusement out of sending you reports and letters."[6]

The real thing is not much different from the scams perpetrated by Wermold, Pym, or Gustav. A CIA spy runner in Western Europe in the 1980s apparently duped his colleagues for five years with lengthy fictitious reports from imaginary European agents on local attitudes toward NATO and skepticism about the U.S. commitment to come to the defense of its European allies in the event of a Soviet attack. Seemingly, the fabricator was a superb writer who had served in high positions in the Washington national security bureaucracy, so he knew the kind of "illegal secret information" that National Security Council staffers lapped up. Ultimately he was defeated by the same combination of factors that undid Wermold, Pym, and Gustav. The legends he developed for his European sources could not withstand the passage of time. There came a point at which he had to open them up to others besides himself, to turn them over to his successor, and more particularly to describe their access and value, and he obviously could not do it. He was pocketing the "salaries" destined for his "agents," which led to his summary dismissal. A "burn" notice was issued for all his reports.

All spy organizations have had to contend with fabricators since the serpent encouraged Eve to eat the apple. In Berlin and Vienna after World War II, the local populations were so poor and desperate, their economies so completely destroyed, and the appetite of the Allies for reliable intelligence information so voracious that cottage industries of fabricators sprang up outside the doors of Allied installations. Much time was spent by intelligence gatherers trying to sort fact from fiction.

Later, prior to the outbreak of the Korean War, in trying to divine the intentions of the North Korean government and whether the U.S.S.R. would support a North Korean invasion of the South, the United States was relying on prisoner-of-war interrogations allegedly coming from captured North Korean soldiers to determine the state of war preparations. It now appears that this intelligence information, which was being filtered through South Korean principal agents, was entirely fabricated by the Soviets who had suborned them.

However, the most bizarre actual case of fabrication during the Cold War was revealed in reports about the Aldrich Ames damage assessment, the effort following his betrayal and incarceration to determine how much harm he had done to U.S. intelligence. Apparently the major compromise had involved supersensitive "blue-border" intelligence reporting from the Soviet Union. The reports owed their name to the distinctive blue border used on the margins to distinguish them from ordinary cable traffic. These documents were handled in a special way and were generally reserved for CIA Directorate of Operations spy reports that contained information of interest to the president and his senior national security advisors.

With reports of this extreme sensitivity, an effort is made to limit distribution only to those officials who have a need to know, and to conceal the actual provenance of the information, while at the same time conveying to the reader some idea of the access of the source. This latter goal is achieved through an artful process controlled by the originator of the report but participated in by expert analysts in the field that is the subject of the report. It is designed to frame a "source description" which gives some indication of the reliability of the source without revealing any identifying details.

The irony of the fabrication in this instance is that it apparently affected the *source descriptions* of the sensitive blue-border reports, not the language of the reports themselves. The official in charge of reports on Soviet issues reportedly became aware after the Aldrich Ames betrayal that many of the blue-border reports on Soviet military and technical developments had come from spies who were under the control of the KGB or GRU. They were thus controlled sources.

The Soviets knew from Ames what targets U.S. intelligence was pursuing and where the gaps were in U.S. knowledge about the Soviet war machine. They therefore determined to fill those gaps and report on those targets in a manner of their own choosing.

Obviously the CIA reports chief who framed the source descriptions did not know about Ames at the time, but he *did* know that much of this SOVMAT intelligence (planes, tanks, military R & D) was being supplied by spies under circumstances in which the Soviets knew that the information was coming to the United States. Yet the source descriptions on the blue-border reports apparently contained *no* indication of this fact. That meant that the president of the United States and his principal national security advisors did not know that this highly important information about Soviet military developments and technical research had *purposefully* been made available to the United States by the Soviet government.

Why did the Soviets do it? To send the United States off on some expensive R & D effort to match a weapons system the U.S.S.R. could not afford and had no intention of developing? It is not clear.

Why did the CIA reports chief fail to indicate his full understanding to the policy makers in the source descriptions? This is a much harder question to answer. The CIA inspector general auditors who uncovered this fabrication reportedly chalked it up to the chief's hubris. The chief simply believed in the truth of the intelligence information contained in the reports he was distributing in the blue-border channel, irrespective of Soviet control of the sources. He knew his subject area well, and he had been around a long time. He was also bureaucratically astute, up to a point. He realized that if he permitted a source description on the reports that suggested the sources were controlled, the substance of the reports would inevitably be called into question. He did not want that to happen.

This was a major breakdown in accountability and the responsibility of command. Apparently, it did not appear in the damage assessment that the reports chief's superiors knew of or countenanced his deception. Excessive compartmentation in the area of Soviet intelligence reports contributed to the disaster. If the damage assessment is accurate, the notion that the commander in chief and his principal advisers were denied the opportunity to decide what this intelligence meant in the context of the way it had been acquired turns the normal order of command authority on its head. It illustrates the danger that in the secret world there will inevitably be a contest between the need to maintain tight security controls over intelligence information and the need to retain a measure of supervisory authority so that this discipline is not abused. Consequently, there is great dependence on the integrity of the officials involved in the enterprise. In the world of espionage, as elsewhere, absolute secrecy corrupts absolutely.

Ten

Sci-Fi

As titillating as it is to watch the latest in spy technology exploding off the screen in a James Bond film, most viewers recognize instinctively that what they are seeing is largely fanciful. Automobiles that turn into saber-wielding weapons or mobile gunships, or briefcases that become sophisticated satellite-enabled communications devices, stretch the imagination of even the most gullible observer. It soon becomes apparent that far from being spy paraphernalia needed for Bond's clandestine mission, it is gadgetry for its own sake. It is there to amaze and overwhelm the viewing audience rather than to get reports home more quickly and safely. Much the same can be said for Tom Clancy's bag of tricks.

It was not always so in the long development of spy fiction. In the early years, technology played a minor role. In *The Riddle of the Sands,* the most advanced technology is Davies's incredibly competent seamanship in dead-reckoning a compass course to the site of the secret German invasion project, and in *The Secret Agent,* it is the bomb that Verloc orders to blow up the Greenwich Observatory, but that blows up his brother-in-law instead. Le Carré and Greene depend on time-honored tradecraft methods to support the spying they tell of: dead drops, book codes, telephone signals, and long surveillance-evasion routes.

None of this does justice to the real world of espionage. And it is the mixture of classic spy methods with the lift brought by technology that distinguishes British and American efforts from the late 1930s on. Real technological achievement, not sci-fi (science fiction), enabled the West to outmaneuver first Hitler's Germany, then the Soviets during the Cold War. This technical edge is still being pursued and maintained in the current war on terrorism.

One has to begin, of course, with the British success in 1940 at Bletchley Park in unraveling the mysteries of the German Enigma code encryption machine that in the "double-cross" system of exploitation enabled the Allies to read and manipulate German military messages during World War II. This extraordinary accomplishment was made possible by the intense interaction of remarkable mathematical minds, some of them just out of university, who threw themselves into the esoteric business of matching random sets of numbers with bits of known or already broken coded text. American code breakers had achieved a similar success with Japanese diplomatic codes prior to Pearl Harbor and followed it with the breaking of the Japanese naval code prior to the Battle of Midway in 1942.

In addition, in 1943, the U.S. Army signals intelligence command mounted an effort to decipher encrypted Soviet communications to Moscow from the Soviet embassy in Washington and consulate in New York, with the initial aim of determining whether the Soviets were preparing to sign a separate peace with Hitler. Instead, over a twenty-year period, using the same techniques employed at Bletchley Park and some of the same mathematical whizzes, the United States read clandestine communications from Soviet spy runners and their American agents, many of whom were highly placed in the U.S. government.

This project, called VENONA, became one of the significant code-breaking successes of the Cold War. It was made possible by the strain of the enormous buildup in Soviet communications traffic created at the start of World War II and the Nazi attack on the Soviet Union. So strapped were Soviet communicators for "one-time pads" with which to supply their worldwide net of agents that they made the irretrievable mistake of reusing discrete pages from previously issued one-time pads. One-time pads operate on the arithmetic principle of matching sets of random numbers *once* between sender and receiver in small groups in a coded message that can then be translated into words by reference to a nonreusable key. The security of the system is dependent upon one-time use of the number groups. If they are used more than once, it is technically possible (if you are a mathematical genius—this was a precomputer age) to develop word-use patterns in context and decipher the text. This is what Army and later National Security Agency (NSA) cryptographers managed to do over years of painstaking effort. In so doing, they uncovered and confirmed the existence of a host of U.S. spies for the U.S.S.R., some of whom had been in place since the early 1930s. Such senior U.S. officials as Alger Hiss, Julius and Ethel Rosenberg, Laughlin Currie, and Harry Dexter White were indisputably shown by VENONA to be Soviet agents.

Sadly, because of the provenance of the information, the sensitivity of the VENONA project prevented sharing of this intelligence with the Congress, the courts, and the American people at the time the messages were being broken out. Further, according to some leading scholars of VENONA, the means by which the intelligence was obtained was considered so sensitive that details of the project were not even shared with the commander in chief, President Harry S. Truman. Of course Truman was informed of the substance of the information the decryptions revealed, but the military Joint Chiefs of Staff, who had line responsibility for the project, deemed that the president had "no need to know" how the intelligence had been obtained because the White House was (like all White Houses since) a leaky place, and the president after all was meeting the DCI on a regular basis, and it was clear that the Soviets had penetrated the Office of Strategic Services (OSS) during the war. If Truman did not in fact know of the existence of the VENONA Project, this was a fateful decision. He never developed the confidence in the bare intelligence facts that the U.S. government had been penetrated by the Soviet Union from the beginning of the New Deal era. He distrusted J. Edgar Hoover's motivation in pushing the "enemy within" line, as well as Senator Joseph McCarthy and the rest of the Republican Right's gleeful assertions that the Democrats were "soft" on Communism.

The effort and ability to decipher the communication codes of potential adversaries begun at Bletchley Park, and continued after World War II in tight coordination between the U.K.'s signals intelligence entity, GCHQ (Government Communications Headquarters), and the U.S.'s NSA, made a huge difference in what the West's spymasters were able to report to their superiors regarding hostile intentions around the world.

In the 1950s, NSA and the U.S. Air Force collaborated to launch large airborne collectors of voice and electronic communications. These converted air force military platforms acted as giant vacuum cleaners sucking in signals from the periphery of the Soviet Union or any closed theater of operations where access to Western observers was restricted and the U.S. needed to know what was going on.

As important as SIGINT was in capturing spy information, the development of the U-2 spy plane and high-resolution overhead photography created a new espionage dimension that further enhanced what the intelligence bureaucracies were capable of reporting to their superiors. It also revealed a degree of flexibility and can-do energy by government that the spy novelists barely hint at.

Spy fiction pits the villain, in the form of a hostile power such as Nazi Germany or the U.S.S.R., or an éminence grise such as Dr. No or Auric Goldfinger, against the United States or Britain in a command-directed technical assault on the West. Not so in the real world. The United States found in the early 1950s that with little intelligence information about Soviet military developments drifting west from human agents in the Soviet Union, due to the extraordinary internal security maintained by Stalin and his successors, a scientific solution had to be worked out to create mechanical eyes and ears, since few human ones were available. The result was an unprecedented secret collaboration among government, academia, and the scientific and industrial communities. President Eisenhower's scientific adviser, former MIT president James Killian, and Polaroid's Edwin Land led a committee of distinguished scientists, academics, and industrialists formed to encourage development of an aircraft that could fly high enough to avoid defensive air measures, but not so high that it could not take photographs of Soviet ground installations which expert photo interpreters could read and make sense of. Enter Richard Bissell as DCI Allen Dulles's special assistant (the same Richard Bissell who was to have such difficulty years later managing the Bay of Pigs covert action).

Bissell had instructions from Eisenhower and Dulles in the mid-1950s to work with Kelly Johnson and the Lockheed "skunk works" in Sunnyvale, California, to bring into existence the U-2 spy plane, a high-altitude gliderlike contraption with an enormous wingspan which could carry a high-resolution camera to photograph the Soviet landmass at an altitude too high for surface-to-air missiles to reach. Working together outside the government bureaucracy and beyond its interfering hand, Johnson and Bissell accomplished their mission, on time and under budget. This prepared the way for the Corona satellite system, which encountered numerous false starts and equipment failures before successfully and regularly contributing to Western knowledge about the Soviet missile test range in Central Asia, and other critical targets, for many years. After the Corona satellite was perfected by the "wizards of Langley"—as scholar Jeffrey T. Richelson labeled its creators in an excellent book on this subject[1]—and followed by birds that carried larger and larger film payloads, research and development went off on a new tack for the next generation of spy satellites. By 1976, the U.S. intelligence community had created the KH-11 satellite, which no longer dumped its payload from outer space for the Air Force to retrieve from some remote ocean location but was supplying digital imagery of the Soviet missile test ranges *in real time* to a ground station in the Washington metropolitan area. The KH-11 received incremental improvements to its payload capacity and to the resolution of its imagery during the succeeding years; it continues to supply the U.S. government with valuable intelligence information on happenings in the Middle East and South Asia. The extraordinary secret cooperation among government, academia, and industry embodied in these successful overhead reconnaissance systems is beyond the imagination of most authors of spy fiction. You have to see the results to believe them.

Almost as impressive as the spy machinery developed by the "wizards of Langley" is the human exploitation of other, more abstruse methods of technical intelligence collection. Through its SIGINT satellite called RHYOLITE, and with the aid of ground stations in Turkey and Iran before the overthrow of the shah, U.S. intelligence assembled enormous amounts of electronic emissions (called ELINT) from the Soviet missile test ranges in Central Asia. Measurement and signature intelligence (MASINT) was also collected and analyzed. These were all learned skills. The CIA's Directorate of Science and Technology (DS&T), created in 1962, pioneered the study and analysis of these exotic signals (called telemetry when lumped together). By the late 1960s and early 1970s, when the United States began to fear that the Soviet Union was seeking technical superiority in the development and deployment of intercontinental ballistic missiles armed with multiple and independently targeted nuclear warheads, the U.S. intelligence community was in a position to accurately assess the probable range, accuracy, reentry vehicle and warhead weight, warhead yield, and type of propellant of each operational Soviet missile. This was an extraordinary accomplishment, only partially comprehended in the technical ability to capture the signals. The analysts had to divine what the signals meant and how they related to one another, and the techniques developed to do so are as impressive as the technological prowess that permitted the capture of signals in the first place. The same could be said for the science of photo interpretation, which stood the U.S. in such good stead at the time of the Cuban Missile Crisis in 1962. Without the photo-interpreter (PI) expertise exemplified by the ability to recognize Soviet intercontinental ballistic missiles (ICBMs) while they were still enveloped in their shipping crates (a pseudoscience the PIs laughingly dubbed "crateology"), President Kennedy might not have had the confidence to conclude that the Soviets were introducing medium- and intermediate-range ballistic missiles to the island.

Fast-forwarding to the present, U.S. intelligence has developed and deployed in Kosovo and in Afghanistan unmanned aerial vehicles (UAVs), popularly known as drones, which have the capacity to fly low over a target area, film it, and return the imagery to their control center in real time. The Afghanistan war revealed a new dimension to this spy capability. CIA UAVs are also offensive weapons with the ability, while circling over the operational theater, to spot, track, and fire with accuracy on remote targets with direction from a central command position. There is little in the spy literature that beats this phenomenon for contributing to the espionage bottom line.

There were other technical achievements in the real world of espionage during the Cold War that Fleming and Clancy could only sit back and admire. The Berlin Tunnel, Operation Gold, has already been discussed. Its audacity at the time it was dug was nearly as important as the take from it. Bill Harvey seemed to be saying, "Okay, if we're unable to get physically close enough to Soviet and East German officials to recruit them, let's listen to their conversations instead." The same might be said for the abortive attempt to tunnel into the new Russian embassy on Mt. Alto in Washington, D.C., that Robert P. Hanssen revealed.

An enormous technical challenge was presented by the *Glomar Explorer* effort in 1974 to raise a disabled Soviet nuclear submarine from the bottom of the Pacific Ocean, from the unheard-of depth of nearly seventeen thousand feet, to examine it for espionage purposes. The secrecy of the project was maintained even though the *Glomar* was a feat of massive and expensive construction over a not inconsiderable period of time. When the *Glomar* was completed and made its way to the location of the sunken sub, it maintained its cover as a research vessel engaged in undersea mining exploration for Howard Hughes. According to published sources, even though the Soviet sub broke up as it was raised from the briny, the sections of its carcass that were recovered yielded a wealth of useful military counterintelligence information about the construction and capabilities of Soviet nuclear submarines.

There were less dramatic but no less significant successes to brag about in the technical world as well. In 1980, Tony Mendez, who headed the disguises branch of the Agency's technical support division (TSD), worked with the Canadian government in Ottawa and the Canadian ambassador in Tehran to exfiltrate six American diplomats who had sought refuge in the Canadian embassy after the U.S. embassy had been over-run by Iranian students in the aftermath of the Ayatollah Khomeini revolution. Mendez succeeded in documenting the six as Canadian members of a commercial film crew, in Tehran to scout out possibilities for a science fiction film on behalf of Studio Six Productions in Los Angeles. After close questioning of one of the team by an Iranian official concerned about his passport photo, the six successfully departed the Tehran airport on January 28, 1980, in TSD-supplied disguises and with TSD-altered Canadian passports to give the Carter administration one of the rare bits of good news on the Iran debacle in the last year of Carter's presidency.

TSD's contributions to the spy effort during the Cold War were not all so successful. There was the matter of MKULTRA described earlier. In addition, the schemes that the CIA came up with to eliminate Fidel Castro in 1960–1961, from spraying his wet suit with noxious substances to poison-dusting his beard or providing him with an exploding cigar, were—as revealed in the Church Committee investigation in 1976—all TSD-originated cockamamy schemes which thankfully were never successfully pursued.

Finally, the project in the late 1960s to turn cats into mobile bugging devices, commonly referred to as "Acoustic Kitty," died a deserved death as technically infeasible, due to a cat's natural interference with the sound pickup from its micro-phones.

These are just random illustrations of the ways in which sophisticated and highly creative uses of Western technology and scientific expertise have been harnessed to enhance the ability of Western spies to do their job. Classical espionage with a technical override has improved agent communications in recent years, with burst radio transmissions in the beginning, succeeded by dedicated satellites. The real thing is just as mind-boggling as James Bond's sci-fi, but it is directed at the spy mission, not at impressing the girls.

In future, the challenges in this area will be extensive. We got a hint of what's in store in Will Smith's recent movie *Enemy of the State*. There we saw a wideband wireless world in which the ability to hack into hostile computers, steal financial data, and manipulate it were all taken for granted. Information warfare is certain to give rise to a spate of new sci-fi spy thrillers, which will doubtless be matched by real-life advances in spy technology.

Eleven

The Game for the
Sake of the Game

His nickname through the wards was "Little Friend of All the World"; and very often, being lithe and inconspicuous, he executed commissions by night on the crowded housetops for sleek and shiny young men of fashion. It was intrigue, of course, he knew that much, as he had known all evil since he could speak, but what he loved was the game for its own sake—the stealthy prowl through the dark gullies and lanes, the crawl up a water-pipe, the sights and sounds of the women's world on the flat roofs, and the headlong flight from housetop to housetop under cover of the hot dark.[1]

Kim's attitude toward the "Great Game" of espionage evolved as he matured, but it always retained this element of love of the enterprise for its own sake.

Later literary incursions into this unconventional approach to spying focus more on the disappearance of a rationale or justification for the undertaking than on the pleasure of the pursuit. Recall the cynicism of Dr. Percival's allusions to the poisoning of the "traitor" Davis in *The Human Factor,* as he discusses the disappearance of ideology in the struggles between the British intelligence service and the Soviets with

KIM AND HIS LAMA

The originator of the fictional Great Game, Kim is Rudyard Kipling's foil for espionage on the Indian subcontinent. Although a European by birth, he could pass for an Indian, and he rendered remarkable service to his various spymasters in a picaresque string of adventures in Kim.

Sir John Hargreaves in clubland. To Graham Greene and John le Carré, this is what spying had come down to—chessboard maneuvers between East and West, signifying little but inflicting unacceptable collateral damage on the bit players misfortunate enough to still be caught up in the game.

It affected both sides. Maurice Castle is victimized by the Soviets with the same attitude Percival and Hargreaves manifested toward Davis:

> "You have never been given the real picture, have you? Those bits of economic information you sent us had no value in themselves at all."
>
> "Then why . . . ?"
>
> "I know I am not very clear. I am not used to whisky. Let me try to explain. Your people imagined they had an agent in place, here in Moscow. But it was we who had planted him on them. What you gave us he passed back to them. Your reports authenticated him in the eyes of your service, they could check them, and all the time he was passing them other information which we wanted them to believe. That was the real value of your reports. A nice piece of deception."[2]

The ironic question that Greene leaves us with is, deception of whom and to what end?

Recall also the frustration of Alec Leamas at what Control had put him through in order to rehabilitate Hans-Dieter Mundt in the eyes of the East German service in *The Spy Who Came In from the Cold*. In the end, so bitter is he at the betrayal of his girlfriend, Liz, that he does not heed George Smiley's command to jump from the Wall to save his own skin.

Earlier, of course, Control had explained the gambit in exactly opposite terms. After asking Leamas to stay out in the cold a little longer so the British service could *discredit* Mundt, Control observes:

> "The ethic of our work, as I understand it, is based on a single assumption. That is, we are never going to be aggressors. . . . Thus we do disagreeable things, but we are *defensive*. That, I think, is still fair. We do disagreeable things so that ordinary people here and elsewhere can sleep safely in their beds at night. Is that too romantic? Of course, we occasionally do very wicked things." He grinned like a schoolboy. "And in weighing up the moralities, we rather go in for dishonest comparisons; after all, you can't compare the ideals of one side with the methods of the other, can you now? . . .
>
> "I mean, you've got to compare method with method, and ideal with ideal. I would say that since the war, our methods—ours and those of the opposition—have become much the same. I mean, you can't be less ruthless than the opposition simply because your government's *policy* is benevolent, can you now?" He laughed quietly to himself. "That would *never* do," he said.[3]

For le Carré, the disgust is cumulative. When the game has become so destructive that it threatens to overwhelm the values that he believes British civilization stands for, Smiley hesitates for a moment before slipping the handcuffs on the treacherous Bill Haydon:

> Then, for a moment, one part of Smiley broke into open revolt against the other. The wave of angry doubt that had swept over him in Lacon's garden, and that ever since had pulled against his progress

like a worrying tide, drove him now onto the rocks of despair, and then to mutiny: I refuse. Nothing is worth the destruction of another human being. Somewhere the path of pain and betrayal must end. Until that happened, there was no future; there was only a continued slide into still more terrifying versions of the present.[4]

Reality is neither as romantic as Kipling suggests in *Kim,* nor as cynical and manipulative as Greene and le Carré paint it in *The Human Factor, The Spy Who Came In from the Cold,* and *Tinker, Tailor.* Spying and running spies have always been *extraordinary* occupations in the literal meaning of the word. Human qualities are called upon that either are not overly developed in many people, or, in the spy or spy runner, become outsized. Discretion, role-playing, and gregariousness are some of the characteristics that come to the fore. Unfortunately, so do a number of less admirable qualities, like manipulation, produced in no small part by the strains of a double life.

Dewey Clarridge refers often in his autobiography to the importance of alcohol as the lubricant for social interaction in diplomatic circles, where the alert recruiter is seeking to lower the guard and loosen the tongue of potential sources of spy information. Abuse of alcohol thus becomes an occupational hazard, destroying families as it did Clarridge's and Aldrich Ames's, and leading to efforts at deception, as in the case of Maurice Castle, who preferred to drink light scotches such as J&B so he could pour himself a double without appearing to.

Nevertheless, somewhere along the line, good spies and spy runners, like Kim, develop a zest for the game of espionage. Their motivations may be primarily monetary like those of Ames and Walker, or ideological like Penkovsky's, but they enjoy the thrill of deception. Or, as in the cases of Kisevalter and Shergold, they thrive on the challenge of keeping their agents alive and productive. Many share in the sentiment expressed by Clarridge at the end of *A Spy for All Seasons* when he asserts that "never once during my thirty-three years at the CIA did I awake in the morning and not want to go to work; I couldn't wait to get there."[5]

The rub comes when the thrill of espionage becomes an end in itself; when the deception and manipulation are used by the spy or spy runner to advance not the established spy mission but the personal and selfish goals of the actor. Obviously the cases of Philby, Ames, and Hanssen exhibit egregious instances of this behavior.

It is hard to credit Kim Philby's statements in his autobiography that he had "no doubt about the verdict of history" that the idea of Communism would triumph in the end. By the time he published his autobiography in 1968, he had seen so many departures from the Communist ideal that intellectually, if not emotionally, he had to have had serious doubts. John le Carré captured Philby's state of mind accurately with his look-alike Bill Haydon. Philby had cleverly worked his way to the top of the heap and with the help of his Soviet masters contrived to stay there. He must have flourished at the summit of power, helping bring on the less experienced American intelligence service, while at the same time keeping an eye out for Soviet interests in the atomic bomb espionage case or the case of the abortive defection of a Soviet diplomat named Konstantin Volkov in Turkey. Some of the thrill for him must have been deception for its own sake, when he alone knew that he had the power to undermine the Allied "rollback" effort in central Europe or make the Americans look bad in their pretension to Western leadership:

> Whether the wartime exchange of British experi-
> ence for American resources really paid off is a mat-
> ter open to argument. What is beyond doubt is that

the decision in favour of cooperation doomed the British services, in the long run, to junior status. That junior status has been a sobering fact for many years. All SIS could do was sit back helplessly when CIA committed the United States Administration to folly with Ngo Dinh Diem or to ridicule in the Bay of Pigs.[6]

Or stab them in the back by betraying them to the Soviets! But anti-Americanism and the Communist ideal are not enough to explain Philby's career of treachery. Philby declares emphatically that he was never a double agent, but he led a double life that taxed him severely, not least because of his responsibility for Burgess and Maclean, whose defections eventually led to Philby's unmasking. The Soviets in Philby's Moscow retirement never accorded him the honor he believed was his due, never regarded him as a senior officer in the Soviet espionage service, as was his wish, or feted him at Dzerzhinsky Square. Perhaps they knew that in the end Philby was in it for himself, that his was a power trip in pursuit of "the game for the game."

Aldrich Ames was never at the center of command like Philby. Nonetheless, pressures were at work on his psyche beyond his apparent need for money to afford his new wife. The CIA inspector general found that Ames, in the course of his successful tour in New York in the late 1970s, often had lunch with the Soviet TASS correspondent accredited there to discuss "matters of mutual interest." In the course of his investigation the IG formed the belief that this is where Ames's slide down the path to betrayal had commenced. Over lengthy boozy lunches, Ames claims, he found much in common between the worldviews espoused by the Soviets and himself. Ames says he began to see the U.S. relationship to the Soviets less in terms of apocalyptic confrontation and more as a need to accommodate understandable nationalist pressures. He also started to be more critical of U.S. foreign policy in the Reagan era, when, at least at the outset, the U.S.S.R. was treated as the "evil empire."

In addition, it is clear that Ames felt underappreciated for his skills as a CIA Directorate of Operations spy runner. He believed that few of his colleagues possessed the knowledge of and familiarity with the Soviet target that he had acquired after working on Soviet matters for twenty years, and he resented being pigeonholed as a terminal GS-14 who would never be a chief of station or be promoted to the senior ranks of the service. His sale of $150,000 worth of U.S. agents to the Soviets after he had liquored himself up sufficiently to make the approach to the Soviet embassy in April 1985 was thus the culmination of a number of frustrations, combined with a loss of perspective that a lifetime in the clandestine world often begets.

The enclosed world of clandestine operations seldom leads its inhabitants to treachery, but the circumstances of living and working in a universe cut off from the outlets of expression available in normal occupations sometimes leads to bizarre behavior. The CIA's Jim Nicholson, who betrayed his knowledge of Soviet operations and young American spy runners to the Soviets after Ames was arrested in 1994, was closer emotionally to his Soviet counterpart in Kuala Lumpur than to members of his own service. Consequently, when he needed money to pay alimony to his wife after their messy divorce, Nicholson went to his Soviet friend and sold secrets before he thought to approach one of his American colleagues for a loan.

Bank tellers and accountants may embezzle funds to vent their career frustrations, automobile workers may sabotage their assembly line to get even with management, prizefighters may throw a fight to win a bet, but spies have another, more calamitous option: they can reveal their secrets to the opposition. After all, they are not readily employable in other occupations after a lifetime of spying, and their world has so narrowed that they don't think of possibilities outside the profession that has been their life to that point. There then arises an additional emotion: the desire to show the top brass that the disillusioned spy has the power to throw a monkey wrench into the whole spy system.

Aldrich Ames encountered all these emotions, often in an inebriated state, and he made judgments that indicated he had lost faith in the goals of the Great Game and was playing it solely for his own account.

Although there are details yet to emerge, the betrayal of Robert P. Hanssen has some of the same earmarks as that of Ames. Hanssen felt himself undervalued in the FBI even though his computer expertise made him indispensable and pulled him into some of the Bureau's most sensitive spy operations against the Soviets and later the new Russian government. He was a loner, and he claimed that he had been drawn to espionage as a career at an early age. But he also needed money to educate his children at expensive Catholic schools.

In the affidavit filed by the U.S. government at the time of Hanssen's arraignment in the spring of 2001, it was disclosed that in a message to his Russian control, Hanssen had stated that he had wanted to be a double agent ever since he had read Kim Philby's autobiography at the age of fourteen. Although, as noted previously, he got the date wrong, that is beside the point; in his head, the idea of leading a double life had already been hatched.

Hanssen was a very different spy from Aldrich Ames. His tradecraft was careful. He never met his Russian spymasters, and he dictated the terms of his engagement; but it seems from his correspondence with the KGB and its successor organization that he experienced moments of isolation from their control, and moments when he wondered whether they appreciated his importance to them and all that he had contributed to their cause.

At the same time, his behavior was exceedingly bizarre. Although he lived well within his ostensible means, retaining a modest home in the Virginia suburbs and driving an old jalopy to work, he apparently spent some of his compensation from the Russians on a Washington, D.C., stripper in an effort to reclaim her from her dismal life. There has not yet been a rational explanation for this act. Nor for the act of videotaping his wife and himself making love for the alleged titillation and amusement of a close friend observing in an adjacent room.

In a further demonstration of the vagaries of human existence, Hanssen's wife apparently caught him out in spying for the Russians in the 1980s, and she took him to their parish church. This matter must have been sui generis for the priest, who heard Hanssen's confession and, dumbfounded by his revelation, advised him to discontinue his spying and give his ill-gotten gains to charity.

Reportedly, when it apprehended Hanssen, the United States was fortunate in having obtained information from a clandestine source who had identified him. Nonetheless, there is a strain in the late messages from Hanssen to the Russians during the time he was on detail to the State Department, as set forth in the government's affidavit, indicating that the pressures of his double life were getting to him. It almost sounds as if he anticipated being identified, and that he might be relieved if it happened.

Probing the thinking and motivation of a Robert P. Hanssen on the basis of the information currently available is a risky business. Nonetheless, according to the affidavits filed in court by the government, there is evidence that Hanssen derived some measure of fulfillment from knowing that he was in a position to greatly injure the national security interests of the United States; that it would vindicate his importance in his own

ROBERT P. HANSSEN
*The highest-ranking U.S. spy
ever to volunteer to work for
the U.S.S.R. during the Cold
War (and Russia after 1991),
Hanssen outdid Aldrich Ames
in the sensitivity of the FBI
secrets he divulged. His
betrayal of his country, the
FBI, and his family was
limitless, and bizarre in its
execution and motivation.*

and the Russians' eyes if he did it; and, given his own disregard of the FBI's counterintelligence capabilities, especially in the information technology field, that he was likely to get away with it for a long time. In a morally lopsided way, Hanssen was playing the game for its own sake regardless of the outcome.

At a deeper, more emotional level, it is clear that Hanssen had been undercut and belittled by his father from an early age. His father had wanted young Hanssen to have the professional career and status as a physician or dentist that modest means and ability had denied him. Consequently, he disapproved of his son's following him into the police and then to the FBI. Hanssen seems to have concluded in his own mind that he was far more intelligent than the average FBI special agent, so he never enrolled in that macho crime-busting fellowship. He, like Ames, was distinctly *not* one of the boys. In his espi-

onage, therefore, he seems to have thrived on the knowledge
that he was deceiving the Bureau by reporting important
secrets to the Russians, who had no idea of his identity and who
communicated with him on his terms. For once in his life, he
felt empowered and in complete control. He wanted to be the
best spy the Soviets had ever run against the West, not because
he believed in Communism, but to prove his self-worth, to
enhance his own self-esteem. As one of his former FBI colleagues noted, "He didn't do it for the gain. He did it for the
game."[7]

The Russians, for their part, knew Hanssen was friendless,
even though ostensibly they did not even know his identity.
They offered the support and friendship Hanssen had never
received from his working colleagues and family. It is apparent
from his final communications to the Russians, around Thanks-
giving in 2000, that he was beginning to worry that with his
diminished access to sensitive information, they might abandon him:

> No one answered my signal at Foxhall. Perhaps you
> occasionally give up on me. Giving up on me is a
> mistake. I have proven inveterately loyal and willing
> to take grave risks which even could cause my death,
> only remaining quiet in times of extreme uncer-
> tainty. So far my ship has successfully navigated the
> slings and arrows of outrageous fortune.
>
> I ask you to help me survive.[8]

Survival was, however, out of the question. In February
2001, Hanssen was apprehended in northern Virginia, near his
home, servicing a dead drop. His final words to his pursuers
were, simply "What took you so long?"[9]

Robert P. Hanssen's motivation for spying for the Russians
has been the subject of intense speculation since his arrest and

imprisonment. He certainly had achieved his goal. He was arguably a far more important spy for the Russians than either Philby or Ames. Why did he do it? A psychiatrist who examined him for his defense and the court has opined that it was due to "an intolerable sense of personal failure."[10] Hanssen himself described it as "fear and rage . . . fear of being a failure and fear of not being able to provide for my family."[11]

Twelve

Spying on Friends and Allies

Although classic spy doctrine makes it clear that there is no such thing as a "friendly" spy service, intelligence agencies have collaborated with one another on matters of common concern from the the spy bureaucracies' earliest days of existence. And there have always been moments that tested the fabric of this "liaison," such as the effort of Mossad in Ignatius's *Agents of Innocence* to get the CIA's help in fingering its spy Jamal Ramlawi as a member of the terrorist organization Black September. Ramlawi's case officer and the chief of station refused to countenance this wrongheaded order from the director of central intelligence and were backed in their insubordination by their superior, who was one of the DCI's principal lieutenants. The DCI was forced to back down and the request from Mossad was dealt with in an indirect way. Nonetheless, the essential point was established: an intelligence service does *not* reveal its spies to another service, even one as close to the United States as the Israeli service was portrayed to be in *Agents of Innocence,* and even when the spy is suspected of conducting terrorist operations against the requester. It's not done. It would be bad for business, because the word would be out in minutes that U.S. intelligence does not protect its own agents. In this upside-down universe of espionage, protecting one's sources is the coin of the realm. Even protecting them from the requests of one's closest allies.

But wasn't the DCI's rejoinder to his refusenik subordinates—that CIA burns spies like Ramlawi every day—the correct one? Aren't the CIA's supposed relations with liaison services like Mossad or with the British more important than one spy? What about the chief of station's observation that the Israelis would not sell out their agent if the shoe were on the other foot?

In the real world, one can begin historically with British efforts in 1940 to bring the United States into the war against the Axis Powers through the mechanism of the office of British Security Coordination (BSC) based in New York City. This office, led by Sir William Stevenson (the author of *A Man Called Intrepid*), far exceeded the brief and latitude for operating in the United States accorded it by J. Edgar Hoover and the FBI by aggressively courting American opinion in opposition to the America Firsters' drive to keep the United States out of the European war, and by countering German interests and propaganda in this country. Whether or not this campaign was winked at by FDR (and it likely was) and driven by Churchill, British intelligence was far more active in pursuit of British interests on American shores than a normal liaison relationship between allied security services would countenance. British intelligence placed stories with American columnists favorable to Britain's wartime plight, opposed and distorted stories favorable to Nazi Germany, and vigorously opposed the promotion and extension of Axis business interests in the United States. In addition, BSC successfully mounted agent operations to sabotage or report on German and U.S. shipping of war-related materiel from American ports to Nazi Germany.[1] This was a clear case of an ally engaged in a life-and-death struggle, determined to do what was necessary to end U.S. neutrality and bring us into the European struggle as we had been in 1917. It was classic political warfare in which a highly skilled but desperate ally used an intelligence liaison relationship to advance its national goals by whatever means necessary.

That leads to the case of Jonathan Pollard. Pollard was a spy for the Israelis in the 1980s, based in Washington, D.C., where he worked for the Office of Naval Intelligence (ONI). He was an American citizen of Jewish ethnicity who believed fervently in the Israeli cause. When he was arrested in 1987, he was shown to have delivered to his Israeli spymaster (who had cover in the Israeli embassy) some of the United States' most sensitive military secrets. He was tried, he pled guilty, and he was sentenced to life imprisonment. Since his incarceration, at regular intervals civil rights activists, pro-Israeli organizations, and prominent American citizens have joined with officials from successive Israeli governments to seek a presidential pardon for Pollard. Their argument is fairly straightforward. Nobody contests that Pollard was a spy. The argument is simply that Israel and the United States are lock-tight allies, that their interests overlap in most aspects of national security, that spying by one on the other is inappropriate but forgivable, and that Pollard has been punished enough for his indiscretions.

Thus far that argument has made no headway with presidents of the United States, even though it was attempted as recently as January 2001, when President Bill Clinton was handing out controversial pardons like popcorn. The members of the U.S. national security establishment—Defense, State, and CIA—are unanimously opposed to clemency for Pollard. Part of the reason is that Pollard is reported to have transferred to the Israelis much more sensitive intelligence than that which would have been acceptable between allies. Also, he apparently has not been truthful about what he did. However, the principal reason for the hard line against a pardon for Pollard in the defense and intelligence agencies is that the national security establishment wants it clear that this kind of behavior between allies, even those as close as Israel, will not be condoned. All recognize that in the spy business it is axiomatic that one tries to achieve a penetration of a rival intelligence service, but among the United States' closest allies the U.S. position is that it is not done. We have agreements to that effect with the intelligence services of our best friends and informal understandings with others, following such flaps as occurred during the French presidential election of 1995.

Indeed, the brouhaha that led to the expulsion of eight American officials from the embassy in Paris in 1995 illustrates the perils of spying on one's friends. It is generally conceded that in the late 1980s the French security services mounted an aggressive campaign of industrial espionage against other Western governments, particularly the United States. American businessmen returned to their Paris hotel rooms to find their briefcases had been rifled and their suitcases messed up. Because the French government at that time held substantial ownership stakes in French aerospace, defense, and high-tech industries, it was anxious to know the negotiating positions or the strategic plans of its private American or multinational competitors. The United States vigorously protested this behavior by the French government, and the French, although they denied it, scaled back their activity. Relations had arrived at a position of cool correctness by the early 1990s.

The French internal security service, a highly competent force called the Direction de la Surveillance du Territoire (DST), was the entity responsible for ensuring that foreign governments did not do on French soil to French companies what the French were doing to them. The DST enjoyed constant and healthy relations with the U.S. government on matters of common concern, chiefly terrorism, organized crime, and third-world operations at that time. In fact, in 1994 the United States had recently tipped off the DST to the whereabouts of the infamous 1960s terrorist "Carlos the Jackal" and was feeling pretty mellow about the relationship.

This was the setting for a summons U.S. Ambassador Pamela Harriman received from French Minister of Interior Charles Pasqua for an interview at his elegant office down the rue du Faubourg Saint-Honoré from the U.S. embassy one evening in December 1994. According to French press reports, Harriman was confronted with a series of photographs showing American "diplomats" meeting with a number of high-ranking and sensitively placed French officials at various locations all over Paris. In addition, Pasqua presented Harriman with written summaries of alleged conversations between the U.S. "diplomats" and their French contacts in which it was evident that the Americans were seeking sensitive information about the current state of French telecommunications and contract negotiations with foreign entities. Pasqua declared this activity to be incompatible with the diplomatic status of the U.S. "diplomats" involved and stated that the French government wanted them out of the country before the end of the year. Subsequent to their interview, most of the detail that Pasqua had presented to Harriman found its way into *Le Monde, Le Figaro,* and other elements of the French press.

Ambassador Harriman denied Pasqua's accusations and stood her ground. But the incident touched off a six-month disruption in relations between the United States and French governments. It turned out that Premier Edouard Balladur was in a losing race for the French presidency (the election was to be held in the spring of 1995), that he and his close entourage had just been accused of trying to bribe a French magistrate on another matter, and that he and his friend Pasqua were probably just trying to divert attention from that scandal by opening up a new front with the Americans.

Leaving aside the reportedly faulty operational security

practiced by the CIA that put the evidence of alleged spying activity in the hands of the DST, the shocking aspect of this flap was that the French government went public with it in the sensational way that it did. Normally, when a spy service is caught out by an allied service with which it has continuous business relations, even if the relations are not close, the matter is handled *between* the services, and generally with discretion. The reason for this is obvious. Why make a big to-do about activity in which you yourself are engaged? There is no such thing as a "friendly" spy service, remember?

In this instance, however, Murphy's Law was at work. A high-profile American attorney with high-tech clients and suspected ties to U.S. intelligence had developed a business relationship with Premier Balladur's son and the DST had found out about the relationship. Although the lawyer in fact was not U.S. intelligence, the French were unconvinced, and, given the proximity to Balladur with the election forthcoming, Pasqua felt he had to act.

In the event, Balladur did not win the election and relations between the French and U.S. governments in all their particulars reverted to their former correct but distant state, but with one significant change. The current U.S. policy with our European allies is that we will continue to work with their intelligence services as before on compatible targets, such as terrorism. This cooperation has been heightened considerably in the wake of the September 11, 2001, terrorist attacks on the World Trade Center towers and the Pentagon.

In order to make a unilateral approach to a European, however, it must be shown that the expected benefit would greatly outweigh the risk before Washington will give the green light. This is how it should be. Spying on friends and allies should not be undertaken unless there is critical gain to be derived and there is no other way of accomplishing the task. Otherwise, the downside is too steep. This would appear to be particularly relevant at a time post–September 11, when the United States is trying to get a grip on the terrorist threat from Osama bin Laden's Al Qaeda network and the Islamist movement more generally. U.S. intelligence will need friends in countries where Americans are regarded as representatives of an infidel culture which is bent on destroying Islam and where, as a consequence, direct contact between U.S. spy runners, even those of Middle Eastern heritage, and Palestinians, Pakistanis, Afghans, and other Middle Easterners is more difficult.

In liaison work with representatives of other friendly intelligence services, however, the temptation will be there to seek a unilateral penetration of such a service when circumstances permit. One is always in need of a window on the thinking of a foreign intelligence service that may appreciate the technical and other support coming from the American side but is facing strong domestic pressures for noncooperation from its own side. Relations between "friendly" intelligence services will blow hot and cold, depending on the times and the issues in play. Except between the oldest and most interdependent allies, the working principle will most often boil down to a quid pro quo exchange in the context of "What have you done for me lately?"

Thirteen

Terrorism and Intelligence

"Listen to me," Barley pleaded. "Just hold on a
minute. I understand. I really think I understand.
You had a talent and it was put to unfair uses. You
know all the ways the system stinks and you want to
wash your soul. But you're not Christ and you're not
Pecherin. You're out of court. If you want to kill
yourself, that's your business. But you'll kill her too.
And if you don't care who you kill, why should you
care who you save?"[1]

This question put to code name Goethe, a disillusioned Soviet
physicist, by his British intelligence contact, when Goethe insists
that his manuscript describing the latest Soviet nuclear weapon
not only become the property of Western intelligence but also
be published in the open scientific literature, thereby dooming
his courier and lover, Katya, is a fitting literary introduction to
the subject of terrorism. The suicide bombers in Israel and the
aircraft hijackers in New York and Washington on September
11, 2001, did not care whom they killed.

"There is only *now*," he explained finally, his voice
not above a murmur. "There is no other dimension
but *now*. In the past we have done everything badly

for the sake of the future. Now we must do everything right for the sake of the present. To lose time is to lose everything. Our Russian history does not give us second chances. When we leap across an abyss, she does not give us the opportunity for a second step. And when we fail she gives us what we deserve: another Stalin, another Brezhnev, another purge, another ice age of terrified monotony. If the present momentum continues, I shall have been in the vanguard. If it stops or goes back, I shall be another statistic of our post-Revolutionary history."[2]

The language above, from John le Carré's *The Russia House*, refers to Soviet Russia, and it refers to the publication of details about a new weapon of mass destruction, but it could as easily refer to the terrorist agenda of Al Qaeda and some Muslim fundamentalists. And the terrorists don't care who they save. The September 11 terrorists' agenda was purely destructive: death to innocent Americans and destruction of symbols of their success and power. It is hard to see how these acts advance the cause of fundamentalist Islam or the opposition groups the terrorists may represent in Egypt, Saudi Arabia, Pakistan, or the Persian Gulf region. They are closer to being the "outrage" that Verloc's pompous Russian diplomat wanted him to perpetrate, in order to stir things up, in *The Secret Agent*.

The intelligence challenge presented by individuals and groups who are willing to sacrifice their lives and those of their closest associates for an abstract or religious ideal is unique and daunting. This is a different phenomenon from terrorism to advance a merely political agenda such as the Irish Republican Army or the Basque separatist movement has practiced. It is harder to track or to crack.

For the reality is that spies and spy runners do not ordinarily intermingle with the people who make up terrorist cells. Terrorists don't frequent Western embassy receptions or hang out with the expatriate community. Obtaining information on Al Qaeda or a line on its adherents is a quasi–law enforcement, investigative function, and one that tests to the utmost the intelligence-gathering resources of intelligence services, both human and technical. Many of the terrorists who bombed the World Trade Center the first time in 1993, the Khobar Towers barracks in Saudi Arabia in 1996, the U.S. embassies in Nairobi and Dar es Salaam in 1998, and the U.S.S. *Cole* in 2000 were recruited from bin Laden's terrorist-training camps and had left no previous imprint in terrorist activity. They were anonymous foot soldiers in service to hatred and destruction.

The only way they are traceable is through acquaintances and neighbors who might observe their comings and goings, or their preparations over a period of time, and regard these activities as suspicious. Further, the observers must be willing to bring that information to the authorities. To bring such a willingness about, spy services and the nations they represent will have to be a lot closer to the grievances that motivate these fundamentalist "wretched of the earth" actors and their middle-class sympathizers than they currently are.

Signals intercepts and overhead reconnaissance will not be of much help, because these terrorist cells either encrypt their communications or don't use devices that are readily interceptible. The members seldom congregate. And it is fascinating and worrisome that, of the nineteen terrorists, many of whom received pilot training in the United States and lived in suburban neighborhoods with their children for part of the two-year period prior to September 11, none was ratted out. Apparently none defected from his mission of death and destruction, and nobody came forward with reports of strange or suspicious behavior that counterterrorist experts could fasten on. The terrorists' operational security dwarfs the precautions taken by the revolutionist chat groups that Verloc regularly convened in *The Secret Agent.*

In this connection, the spy services of the West are long overdue for improvement. As Auric Goldfinger observed to James Bond: "Mr. Bond, they have a saying in Chicago: 'Once is happenstance. Twice is coincidence. The third time it's enemy action.' "[3] Many thoughtful observers believe it is high time for the United States and its principal allies to take the religious terrorist threat for what it is: a wide-ranging assault on the cultural and economic assumptions of the West and the globalism that is its manifestation.

Ironically, this will require a reversion to the tradecraft and technique of an earlier era of espionage—that of the Great Game, before the gadgetry and sophistication of overhead photography and instant wireless communications. Spy services will have to become reacquainted with the world of *Kim* with its ground truth: Kim's ability to pass as a Hindu native; his knowledge of Pathan, Tibetan Buddhist, Bengali, and local Muslim cultures and practices; and his unerring instinct for operating in the night-soil world with its poverty, superstition, and ignorance.

Fourteen

The Rogue Elephant

After we have considered the numerous ways in which the power of a state is mobilized to spy on the plans, intentions, and activities of another, or to direct covert action to influence or overthrow it, the question naturally arises: Who is responsible for authorizing and supervising this extraordinary activity? To whom do the spymasters report? By whom and by what are they directed and controlled?

In the case of the CIA, at the time of the Church Committee investigation in 1975–1976, Senator Church urged the theory that no superior governmental authority was in charge. Presidents of the United States either had abdicated responsibility or had known too little about what the CIA was doing to exercise meaningful control, he observed. The Agency was thought to be plotting the assassination of foreign leaders, opening the mail of U.S. citizens, testing its own employees with mind-expanding drugs without their knowledge, and infiltrating antiwar demonstrations in the United States ostensibly without White House knowledge or approval. He called the CIA a "rogue elephant," and although he had to step back from this characterization when it was revealed in the committee's final report that U.S. presidents had in fact known of and ordered many of the activities, including the assassination plots, to which the committee objected, nonetheless the accusation stuck.

The idea of the intelligence agencies operating on their own account, outside the laws which created them, dominated congressional thinking in the aftermath of the Church investigation in 1976 and gave rise to the creation of legislative committees in the House and Senate to oversee the agencies' activities. In time the business of espionage and covert action became a shared responsibility between the executive and legislative branches of government in the U.S., much like the conduct of foreign affairs and national defense. Given the number of persons who thereby became entitled to share the secrets of espionage and covert action, many would argue that the possibility of keeping these secrets when the underlying spy operation was sensitive *and* controversial diminished considerably.

It was not always so, in other spy regimes or in other times, in fiction or in reality.

In the beginning, in defense of empire in the nineteenth century, the British intelligence service used human spies as just another foreign policy tool to keep Russia and France out of the Indian subcontinent, as in *Kim,* or to frame a defense to keep the German navy from dispatching small boats to attack the vulnerable East Anglian coast, as in *The Riddle of the Sands.*

SIGINT was used by Britain in the same way, to intercept the Zimmermann telegram in 1916 and give it to the U.S. government as an inducement for it to join the war on the side of the embattled European allies. In similar fashion, a U.S. effort to decrypt the Japanese naval code in the 1920s was carried out by Herbert Yardley and the "Black Chamber" in the U.S. Department of State. It was all very patriotic, sometimes highly amateurish, and on the whole not very well organized. It was with the onset of World War II, and the extraordinary British achievement of capturing the German Enigma machine and then cracking the code in the top secret Ultra project, that the West could see for the first time the extraordinary advantage that systematically reading another nation's secrets could bring in wartime. So greater efforts in terms of manpower, treasure, and technical sophistry were expended on espionage during the war by all the principal combatants.

With the prominent exceptions of Ultra and its U.S. offshoots, the effort against the Japanese diplomatic and naval codes before and during the war, and the VENONA Project to read Soviet diplomatic traffic, which began in 1943, major institutionalized regimes dedicated to obtaining strategic advantage through technical and human espionage awaited the Cold War to flower and become fully developed.

At least, this appears to have been the case in the West. John Lewis Gaddis makes the argument in his excellent book, *We Now Know*,[1] that Josef Stalin began a concerted effort to recruit sources in the ruling elites of the United Kingdom and the United States in the 1930s with the acquisition of the Cambridge Five, along with Alger Hiss, Harry Dexter White, and others in President Franklin D. Roosevelt's inner circle. As a nearly clinical paranoid, Stalin always believed that the British and the Europeans, and later the Americans, would combine to try to undermine the Soviet state. Stalin exerted absolute control over his intelligence services, using them to maintain the authority of the Communist Party of the Soviet Union domestically, as well as to extend its influence abroad. He brooked no opposition and employed his own analytical biases in interpreting the raw intelligence reports he was receiving from his spies in the West. For example, Stalin never believed that the European powers and the U.S. would ally themselves permanently with a Bolshevik regime to fight the Nazis, despite numerous spy reports to the contrary. He rejected intelligence reports that Hitler was preparing to shred the Stalin–Ribbentrop Pact in 1941, until he could see with his own eyes the panzers advancing on the Russian border. Because he never fully trusted the intelligence he received from his spies, Stalin undercut his own effort to penetrate Western governments by extending the devastating purges of the late 1930s to the intelligence elements of the Soviet state. This resulted in the recall to the U.S.S.R. of many of the same master spies and illegals who had recruited and run Stalin's U.K. and U.S. informants.

As he did in his home precincts, Stalin ruled his European empire with great cruelty and a tight fist. Churchill's "iron curtain" appellation justly described the barrier Stalin had erected between the Soviet Bloc and the West, and Western intelligence was at a severe disadvantage in attempting to penetrate that barrier during the early Cold War years. In effect, espionage became a paradigm for the period. We were all at a disadvantage in the West trying to look inside the Soviet Bloc. Meanwhile, with Stalin's head start in espionage efforts against the West, the Soviet Union appeared to be presiding over a string of intelligence successes during this period, such as the theft of U.S.-U.K. atomic secrets.

Recognizing the difficulty of penetrating the Soviet state, American and British political leaders directed their intelligence minions during the late 1940s and early 1950s to fight fire with fire. Do to the Soviets what they are doing to us, they ordered. It is from the National Security Council directives embodying this Cold War rallying cry that many of the CIA excesses later revealed in the Church Committee investigation received their spiritual blessing, if not their actual start.

It is also from the directives and atmospherics emanating from this period that a cynical view of espionage began to appear in spy fiction. Control could order Alec Leamas into the operation to preserve Mundt without informing him of his actual role and Liz Gold's part in it, in *The Spy Who Came In from the Cold*. Percival and Hargreaves could eliminate Davis to preserve MI6's reputation with the American cousins, so their cooperation with British intelligence would be uninterrupted, in *The Human Factor*. And the director of central intelligence could contemplate shopping the CIA's penetration of Fatah to the Israelis, to assuage their thirst for revenge after the Munich Olympics killings, in *Agents of Innocence*. Spy novelists asked the question that legislative overseers and Western populations would later ask, whether in adopting the tactics and brutality of the Cold War enemy, the West might be undermining the democratic principles that distinguished our system of government from theirs. Major intelligence fiascoes like the Bay of Pigs seemed to validate these concerns.

Luckily, there followed a time when the West succeeded in making several classic espionage penetrations of the Soviet Union in the enlisting of agents like Pyotr Popov and Oleg Penkovsky, whose services were invaluable during the Cuban Missile Crisis. These tended to eclipse the dreadful losses of human capital in the maw of Stalin's repressive machine during the unrelieved failure of Operation Rollback. In contrast, during the regime of Nikita Khrushchev, after Stalin's death, the ideological appeal of Soviet Communism to spies like Hiss or Philby had diminished considerably. Khrushchev had no spies on the ground in Washington in the fall of 1962 to report on the deliberations in President Kennedy's inner circle about the United States' intentions with regard to the Soviet missiles in Cuba. He had no American Penkovsky.

Until the Vietnam War and Watergate, U.S. intelligence always appeared to be embodied in the American mind by the CIA and the person of the director of central intelligence. This was in fact no longer an accurate perception by the late 1960s, if it ever had been. The U.S. signals intelligence effort was consolidated in the establishment of the National Security Agency (NSA) in the final days of the Truman administration in 1952, and the overhead reconnaissance mission, "spies in the sky," was centered in the secret National Reconnaissance Office (NRO) in 1960. The Defense Intelligence Agency (DIA), originally conceived to embrace all intelligence activities of the Department of Defense, was created in 1961.

The CIA, however, continued to get most of the attention from Americans and spy novelists fixated on U.S. intelligence, because of its primary responsibility for human spy operations and large covert action projects. That's why the publication in December 1974 and January 1975 in the *New York Times* of a series of articles by Seymour Hersh, detailing the abuses of power and the infringement of civil liberties of U.S. citizens by the FBI and CIA, produced such an explosion. The guardians of U.S. liberty against the stealthy and all-out assault mounted on them by Stalin and monolithic Communism were shown to be lawbreakers themselves. The consensus which had existed from the earliest days of the Cold War to fight the spread of godless Communism had been shattered by the perceived petering out of the direct Soviet threat, the tragedy of the Vietnam War, and the criminal behavior of an American president in the Watergate break-in. Now Hersh and the *Times* had revealed that Americans were being victimized by the forces they had unleashed to counter the Communist threat.

While overdrawn, these accusations, as investigated and publicized by the congressional committees, gave rise to a very different optic being applied thenceforth to U.S. intelligence. The CIA had lost its special place in the eyes of many Americans. The change ensured the popularity of a number of spy novels that chronicled the seamy "reality" of espionage, which destroyed lives and pursued operational success at great human cost, such as the le Carré, Greene, and Clancy texts considered previously. Espionage became a world populated less by unsung national heroes than by power freaks, character misfits, and clandestine obsessives who often appeared to pursue the game for the sake of the game, rather than from patriotic motives. To a very real extent, it took the end of the Cold War and the emergence of a new, random, stateless threat like terrorism to create a renewed respect for and interest in spies and spying.

Meanwhile, in the final two decades of the Soviet Union's existence, spy wars between the great powers were conducted in exchange for an ageless medium: money. Ideology was out. American turncoats like William Kampiles, the Walker family, Edward Lee Howard, Earl Pitts, Aldrich Ames, Jim Nicholson, and Robert Hanssen may have had minor grievances against their spy service employers, but their principal need and thus motivation was cash, and plenty of it. It is ironic that with the U.S.S.R. on a downward spiral, the full extent of which neither the West with all its espionage resources, nor in all likelihood the Soviet leadership itself, fully comprehended, spy wars heated up to a pitch not seen since the earliest days of the Cold War. With the near-total collapse of the Soviet economy and the dispersal of the Soviet state in 1991, it is now fashionable to minimize the threat posed to the West by the U.S.S.R. in its final stages. Historians and spy novelists will note, nonetheless, that Moscow remained possessed of a fearsome nuclear arsenal pointed at the West until Boris Yeltsin took over, and it still holds dominion over an awesome array of nuclear weapons.

It is true, however, that the Soviet intelligence services came under real strain in the late 1980s, as the Soviet state began to loosen up internally and in Eastern Europe. The KGB and then the SVR continued to spy vigorously against the "principal adversary," but with perhaps a diminished attention to operational security. Certainly Aldrich Ames believed his spymasters put him in jeopardy by rolling up so quickly the U.S. agents he betrayed to them. Nevertheless, KGB influence remained a powerful force in Russian governance even after the disintegration of the Soviet Union. Vladimir Putin is but the latest Russian leader formed by experience in the intelligence world.

He follows Lavrenty Beria, who contended for the top job after Stalin, and Yuri Andropov, who held it for a short time after Leonid Brezhnev. That compares with George H. W. Bush, who had been director of central intelligence for a year in 1976–1977, the only U.S. president ever to come from the professional intelligence ranks.

The CIA, the NSA, the NRO, the DIA, and the FBI all played significant roles in bringing the Cold War to a successful conclusion for the West. Under the direction of Presidents Carter, Bush, and Reagan and with the concurrence and prodding of a U.S. Congress now in the loop, U.S. intelligence performed credibly in the end in alerting its political masters to the ongoing threat to the West from the Soviet nuclear arsenal and in containing the spread of Soviet power to Angola, Afghanistan, and Central America. It did less well in predicting the Soviet Union's economic and institutional collapse.

Perhaps the role of U.S. human spies in the Cold War is best and most accurately described in a self-styled "novel of the CIA," published in 2002, entitled *The Company.* In it, a young American spy runner who has been captured by the Soviets is swapped in Berlin for a Soviet spy caught in the United States. In a ritualized do-si-do as ancient as the Cold War, the two spies pass each other on a bridge, exchanging a few false pleasantries as they march to their separate destinations. The CIA officer, a second-generation spook, then falls into the arms of his waiting girlfriend and extends a hand to his father:

> "I broke the eleventh commandment," said the young man. [Meaning: "Thou shalt not get caught."]
>
> "We don't think it was your fault," the other man replied. "The way they pulled out his wife and daughter on a moment's notice, then brought him home a day later—given how the game played out it all begins to look very premeditated. They must

have become suspicious of him in Washington and then just outplayed us. You were sent on a wild-goose chase."

"I lost my Joe, Dad. He's dead. Jim Angleton was right—I was too green. I must have gone wrong somewhere—"

The three started toward the Jeeps. "I know how you feel," remarked the man with binoculars. "I've been there a bunch of times. It's the downside of what we do for a living."

"Is there an upside?" the girl demanded.

"Yes, there is," he shot back. "We're doing a dirty job and we get it right most of the time. But there's no way you can get it right every time." The fog was rolling in off the river, imparting a pungent sharpness to the night air. "What keeps us going, what keeps us sane," he added, talking to himself now, "is the conviction that if something's worth doing, it's worth doing badly."[2]

Le Carré described a happier outcome in *Smiley's People* when Smiley went to a similar bridge to greet his longtime adversary and Soviet master spy, the defecting Karla.

Fifteen

Life After Spying

In a dying civilization, political prestige is the
reward not of the shrewdest diagnostician but of the
man with the best bedside manner. It is the decora-
tion conferred on mediocrity by ignorance.[1]

So writes Latimer, the narrator of Eric Ambler's *A Coffin for
Dimitrios*, about Dimitrios's first political-action intrigue, rig-
ging the election of Prime Minister Stambulisky in Macedonia in
1923. Stambulisky possessed that bedside manner, and it was
Dimitrios's task on a fee-for-service basis to get him the job. It
didn't work.

From Macedonia, Dimitrios moves on to Belgrade in 1926;
his assignment is to help master-spy-for-hire Grodek steal the
Yugoslav plans to mine the Adriatic sea lanes on behalf of Italy.
It is the Yugoslav intention to make the Adriatic impenetrable
for the Italian navy in revenge for Italy's seizure of Fiume
(Rijeka) from Yugoslavia after the First World War. The relevant point is that the Italians have contracted out their espionage to Grodek rather than doing it themselves. This gives
them more than plausible deniability, since Grodek, if caught,
is known to work for any nation that pays him best—strictly a
commercial operation.

The operation goes like clockwork, Grodek discovering and

KIM AND HIS LAMA

suborning a greedy Serb named Bulic, who works in the Yugoslav Ministry of Marine, and his greedier wife. Grodek brings in Dimitrios as a suave, wealthy industrialist who introduces the Bulics to the pleasures of the high life, wining and dining them and swindling them at a fancy Belgrade gambling den. When Dimitrios finally pulls the string on Bulic and blackmails him into stealing the Yugoslav plan to mine the Adriatic, it is left for Grodek to collect the goods and pay off his helper Dimitrios. But Dimitrios refuses his scripted role and tries to steal the plans for himself to sell to the Italians. Grodek is forced to denounce him to the French, and so neither ends up making any money.

Is this the way spying for hire works out in the real world? It did for the CIA's Ed Wilson, who sought to sell restricted military equipment and munitions to the Libyans in the late 1960s. He was caught, tried, and imprisoned. James McCord, a retired CIA security official, suffered a similar fate in his unhappy role as chief of the Watergate burglars. More than one unhappy ending has befallen ex-spies who have tried to profit in the commercial world from the knowledge and practices that they learned in their clandestine careers. Of course, traitors like Philby, Penkovsky, Ames, and Hanssen often end up in front of a firing squad, in jail, or as displaced persons in the country for which they spied.

For the underlying truth is that while the skills learned in breaking the laws of other countries to serve the national security interests of Uncle Sam are not legally actionable in the official realm, they often are so when employed on behalf of a private party in the commercial sector.

This has always been a sore point for American spies who see the lucrative jobs that retired military and foreign service officers have worked themselves into with their foreign contacts, often by laying the groundwork while still on active duty. Somehow, the American spies complain, the U.S. government does not look in so kindly a fashion at efforts by retiring spies to strike a deal with friendly foreign intelligence agencies to provide consulting services after their employment at the CIA has ended.

This issue came to a head in the early 1990s when a senior U.S. spy runner in a major world capital agreed to go into private business with a senior official of the local spy service with which he was in liaison after he, the American, retired. The problem presented was twofold. First, since the U.S. official had made this postretirement arrangement when he was still on the active rolls, did this represent a conflict of interest that might have tempted the American spy to say more to his future partner than he should have while he was still on active duty? Second, is it appropriate for senior U.S. spy runners who may have had access to some of America's more sensitive inside information to be perceived as being in partnership with foreign officials, potentially using that knowledge for private advantage?

The U.S. Congress did not struggle with this question for very long. They directed the CIA to impose postemployment restrictions for senior officials who had held policy-making responsibilities in the Agency enjoining them from going to work for foreign governments for three years after the termination of their Agency employment.

This restriction was tightened further in the spring of 1998, after it became known that a controversial Lebanese-American businessman named Roger Tamraz had tried to enlist the help of a serving U.S. intelligence officer to establish his bona fides with the Office of the Vice President of the United States in competing for U.S. government support for an oil pipeline project in central Asia. The call on behalf of Tamraz had been orchestrated by a former CIA officer who had been on Tamraz's payroll for a time. The affair had the smell of an improper mix of private and government business. While there was nothing illegal about putting in a good word for a political friend who had helped the government in times past with sensitive reporting, the notion that the call had come over the transom from an active-duty intelligence operative, and been triggered by a call from a former intelligence officer who had then been on contract with the interested businessman, gave the aroma of overripe cheese to the entire proceeding. It also probably doomed the nomination of Tony Lake, the president's former national security advisor, to be director of central intelligence, since the thoroughness of his supervision of outside contacts with the National Security Council (NSC) staff became a political issue because of Tamraz's intervention.

In any event, it is now clear in the U.S. intelligence world that senior ex-spies will not be permitted to go to work for foreign governments to which they were accredited while on active duty, or to represent the interests of their former agents or collaborators before the government for a period of three years after termination of their government service. Retired spies are not to be regarded in the same way as defeated congressmen or former cabinet members. Their right to make a living out of what they learned in government, and about government, is severely restricted. They are constrained to write books which must be cleared before publication by the intelligence authorities they are writing about; or teach a generation of students that prior to September 11 was no longer drawn to public service, even spying, or throw their intelligence pearls before business clients who just want to know if they are running any undue personal risk in doing business in country X.

In many ways, the best model for a full life after spying was set by the CIA's first general counsel, Lawrence Houston, an inveterate Chesapeake Bay sailor. When he retired from the Agency, he just hoisted sail and took off.

As le Carré notes in *The Russia House*, "spying is normality taken to extremes."[2]

Conclusion: Myth or Reality—Does Espionage Have a Future?

The work of an agent in the Intelligence Department is on the whole extremely monotonous. A lot of it is uncommonly useless.[1]

These words of Somerset Maugham, written in 1927 as part of the preface to *Ashenden,* in which he was trying to set forth in fictional terms his experiences in British intelligence during World War I, could have been uttered by spies from any country—and their spymasters—during any historical period. The question is, is the Great Game worth the candle?

The British government believed so in Kim's time, because informers like Kim allowed the colonial authorities to keep track of efforts by other great powers such as France and Russia to infiltrate the more remote rajistans in the Indian subcontinent and suborn the local potentates. Her Majesty's Government would then move in and give the disloyal maharajah the boot. You could not obtain this information on the diplomatic circuit or from friendly sources in the administrative centers. You had to be in the "outback," as Kim was trained to be, to spot the invaders.

Likewise, Davies and Carruthers were playing for keeps in *The Riddle of the Sands.* If the Kaiser had been permitted to embark upon his putative scheme to attack the vulnerable East

Anglian coast of Britain with an armada of small warships steaming through the sand berms of the Frisian Islands, it would have been a monumental disaster for which the British were seemingly totally unprepared. Davies's volunteer spy effort to put his extraordinary seamanship to work for a trusting, complacent, perhaps even somnolent Britain justified in his mind the enormous personal risk he and Carruthers were taking.

If Richard Hannay had not unraveled the mystery of the Black Stone or prevented the hawk-hooded German spy from embarking for his homeland with the secrets of the high-level consultation between the British and the French military which he had penetrated, war between Britain and Germany would have begun even sooner in *The Thirty-nine Steps*.

At a later time, Marko Ramius's determination in *The Hunt for Red October* to bring the latest Soviet boomer submarine with its new silent "caterpillar" propulsion system to the United States was an intelligence coup of the first order. It clearly justified the existence of an intelligence establishment geared to encourage and exploit this kind of defection. Not only would the United States be alerted to the latest Soviet underwater ballistic missile threat, but, if it had in its possession the new silent propulsion system to pore over, a key countermeasure might be devised.

Even Alec Leamas, as he raged inwardly at his manipulation by Control in *The Spy Who Came In from the Cold,* recognized that East German spy chief Hans-Dieter Mundt was of great value as a source to British intelligence. Leamas could intellectually accept the scheme to save Mundt by destroying Fiedler and Liz, and ultimately himself, although he abjured the cockeyed value system that brought it about.

Nevertheless, there are dissenting voices in the spy literature, and not merely on moral grounds.

Conrad's disdain for the entire universe of central European agents provocateurs in London and Paris at the beginning of the twentieth century is palpable in *The Secret Agent*. He treats it as no surprise that the Russian embassy wants "activity" after eleven years of paying Verloc for meaningless bits on the plotting by superannuated émigrés who have no intention of doing more than talking.

By contrast, Greene and le Carré describe meaty spy operations. There is an object to the exercises they describe. There is a mission to satisfy. Many of the operations they recount have a counterintelligence thrust, such as the efforts to capture the mole Bill Haydon or the spymaster Karla or the leaker Davis/Castle. The observation by Greene and le Carré, however, is that the pursuit of the "Great Game" has corrupted the players. In portraying the British spy system's willingness to sacrifice a life to remain in the good graces of the American "cousins" in *The Human Factor*, or the "cover your bottom" antics of Control's successor, Percy Alleline, and PermSec Oliver Lacon in enlisting George Smiley to turn the Circus upside down to find the mole when SIS has oversold the product of the source Merlin in *Tinker, Tailor*, Greene and le Carré are saying simply that the spy system has become thoroughly rotten. The methods of the Soviet opposition have been incorporated into MI6 and its leaders have lost their bearings. In their quest to obtain and hold power, Britain's spymasters are no different morally than their totalitarian adversaries. Intelligence information is an afterthought. The Great Game is being played for personal stakes and for the sake of the game alone.

David Ignatius explores a different angle in *Agents of Innocence*. Like Greene in *The Quiet American*, he believes that U.S. intelligence promises too much. In seeking peace in the Middle East or halting the advance of Communism in Southeast Asia, the United States is extending a hand that it reserves the right to withdraw eventually. Local people hear more than what U.S. spy runners are saying. They yearn to believe that the Yanks are there to make their lives better and that they are prepared to stay the course. When the time comes and the Americans depart, their agents and collaborators get left behind. The locals have changed position in reliance on a promise, express or implied, that U.S. spy runners would make their lives better, and when that promise fades, they are worse off than if they had never built up their hopes.

Reality is different and is related more to the organizational norms that spying for a bureaucracy demands. Espionage occurs when governments are unable to acquire by other means information they deem important for national survival. Germany was not going to tell Britain of its plans to invade East Anglia, nor were the Soviets, years later, about to reveal their intention to place ballistic missiles in Cuba. Western governments would be forced to discover these intentions on their own. Quite clearly the intentions would not be manifested in any openly available documents, and no official who was "in the know" would be authorized to reveal such information. The West would have to steal it, hence a return to Philby's definition of intelligence as collecting "secret information from foreign countries by illegal means."

The collection itself might be done technically, by electronically intercepting communications or photographing installations, or it might occur the old-fashioned way, with the aid of a human spy. The point is, this is the realm of extraordinary measures, justified in a constitutional democracy only as self-defense, and only by the gravity of the threat and the absence of suitable alternatives.

Given the challenges to Western democracies in the twentieth century posed by Nazi Germany and the Soviet Union, both of which wanted to expand their dominions at the expense of their neighbors, and both of which controlled the flow of information internally in totalitarian fashion, spying became an accepted practice to pierce their armor and seek indications of their intentions. There was very little dissent about this state of affairs from 1938 until the demise of the Soviet Union in 1991.

At the same time, these were exceedingly difficult targets, which is why the spy literature that has grown up around the effort to penetrate Hitler's Germany and Stalin's Russia is so rich. Readers recognized the need for and the difficulty of playing by "Moscow Rules" to obtain intelligence information.

Success did not come easily. When Allen Dulles hung out his shingle in Bern, Switzerland, during World War II, in the hope of enticing some of his prewar German contacts who could still travel across the border to reveal the contemporary state of Nazi war preparedness and the high command's attitude toward the Führer, he was engaged in a sensitive intelligence-collection task of the highest importance to the Allies' plans for the invasion of Normandy.

Likewise, years later, in 1962, when Kisevalter and Shergold were debriefing Penkovsky about Khrushchev and his relationship with the Soviet general staff, the payoff was immediate and critical. Penkovsky's observations about Khrushchev's isolation from the military high command and in the Politburo, and his tendency to shoot from the hip, folded right into Ambassador Llewelyn Thompson's advice to President Kennedy during the Cuban Missile Crisis. Combined with Penkovsky's analysis of the performance characteristics and limited availability of the medium- and intermediate-range ballistic missiles Khruschev was seeking to install in Cuba, this spy information gave JFK the confidence to try using a naval blockade to give Khrushchev an opportunity to step back from the brink, before an all-out American invasion was mounted.

Thus intelligence from human spies can make and has made a substantial difference in the real world to decision makers confronting the hostile activities of foreign countries. The trick is to know when it is needed and how to use it, if you are fortunate enough to obtain good spy information on a timely basis.

For spying is expensive, in both human and institutional terms. It is not something that Americans in particular are very comfortable with in peacetime (or at any time, for that matter), absent a rival with the capacity to destroy the United States with nuclear weapons or terrorists prepared to randomly attack our people and institutions. Given America's traditional mistrust of European back-alley machinations and secrecy, espionage is a hard sell to a public used to confronting its adversaries up front and without guile.

There is some evidence that this national openness of character diminishes the appeal of spying as a career to young Americans not faced with an implacable enemy like Nazi Germany, the Soviet Union, or Al Qaeda, or inhibits the development of the ruthlessness necessary to the making of an effective spy runner. Dewey Clarridge bemoaned the declining appeal of the clandestine service in 1984 to America's best and brightest in *A Spy for All Seasons*. His comment may be overdrawn, however, as each generation responds differently to the call for national service. The Cold War made it plain in Clarridge's time that espionage was a key element in the United States' national defense. Perhaps the specter of September 11, 2001, and the challenge of preventing future terrorist acts will do the same for spying in the current era. Indeed, press reports point to a recent upsurge in CIA applications, a phenomenon I can attest to among my students.

Accountability is necessarily difficult in the spy world, and is often delayed by virtue of the rules of engagement. Compartmentation of knowledge about a spy operation in order to preserve secrecy and protect spies identities and methods makes identification of a problem slower and less certain or effective. The clandestine world of spies and spy runners is a universe apart. It has its own rules, its own code of behavior, its own heroes. It is hard for an outsider to penetrate this inner sanctum.

Furthermore, the inhabitants of this special world become cut off and isolated themselves. The difficulty of maintaining several identities at once increases with time: the spy runner may be a diplomat by day, but a side-street wanderer by night. The spy may be a seemingly loyal, dull, and hardworking government functionary by day, but a screaming risk taker by night, prowling city parks for a suitable dead drop or photographing documents in a cramped hideaway for delivery to his control the next day. The toll of such a double or triple life is heavy. Some spies and spy runners drink to excess or womanize. They have good years and bad. Their families and close associates suffer and are often blown apart. They make operational mistakes. Sometimes they forget where they are and use the same manipulative techniques and half-truths developed to recruit spies on their colleagues *inside* the spy organization.

In the end, espionage is pick-and-shovel work. It is often the least efficient way to accomplish a task, with requirements for clandestine meeting sites, evasion routes to avoid detection, cover stories, and coded communications standard operating procedure. If it were possible to accomplish the same tasks by open means, it would be hundreds of times easier, less expensive, and less likely to produce human detritus. That's why spying should remain the avenue of last resort for representative democracies seeking to protect their national security. It is not a reliable, off-the-shelf response to many intelligence problems.

With the passing of the Cold War, have we seen the last of the spy novel and the need for spies and spying? What challenges are presented to Western governments in the twenty-first century by acts of international terrorism; proliferation of biological, chemical, or nuclear weapons; or crime that will call for a response that includes espionage? And what will be the impact on spying of new information technology and the possibility of information warfare?

Ironically, given the contentious history of relations between the two disciplines, there has been a necessary rapprochement between law enforcement and the spy services. Catching terrorists requires using informants who may themselves have blood on their hands, and this may create the need to involve the criminal justice establishment to grant approvals. This is a particularly tricky issue in the United States, where the CIA by statute has no "police, subpoena, law-enforcement powers or internal-security functions."[2]

In addition, the traditional goal of supplying timely intelligence to the policy maker may be supplemented in the case of terrorist or criminal information with the need to bring a criminal prosecution. That means that spy runners in the twenty-first century will have to become adept at collecting data that can be authenticated for possible presentation to a court of law. Spies may have to be prepared to testify. They may need to be protected from retribution like any other critical witness in a criminal trial.

This is a brave new world for Western intelligence agencies. It will demand in most instances close cooperation with the host spy service where the incident occurred or the perpetrator can be found. Liaison relationships thus become crucial, doubtless sometimes leading to overinvolvement with local brigands like Manuel Noriega in Panama and, reportedly, Vladimiro Montesinos in Peru. Nonetheless, there is a long history of Western law enforcement dealing successfully with the criminal challenges of mob violence, terrorism, and drug trafficking domestically, so there is ample room for collaboration and a sharing of spy expertise with the gumshoes. It will just be a different world.

The impact on the literature will be equally ironic. Having had their beginnings in the detective fiction or "policiers" of the nineteenth century, spy novels will go full circle and return to their origins in crime, but without national borders, and in many instances without roots in struggles between nation-states. The Osama bin Ladens and Kim Jong-Ils of this new universe of spy fiction will have more in common with Dr. No and Goldfinger than with Karla or Jamal Ramlawi.

The Great Game will be played with modern information technology as well. A spy service would not have to have pursued an officer in Saddam Hussein's entourage to effect a penetration of the Iraqi brain trust but instead might have found an inconspicuous street urchin who could place, somewhere near the seat of power, a microscopic transmitter to a satellite. As one of my students demonstrated in a term paper two years ago, it would have been theoretically possible to put Osama bin Laden out of business by electronically diverting all of the assets from his Swiss bank account rather than trying to find him in the desert with a cruise missile.

The technical aids to espionage are bounded only by the limits to the imaginations and resources of the spy runners who employ them. Unfortunately, the bad guys against whom this new technology will be directed will also have access to electronic weapons and countermeasures of their own. The current history of espionage is a tale of official spy services falling behind the private sector in the development of cheap encryption devices, for example, and the world's computer warfare experts don't all work for Uncle Sam. This should spark an outpouring of sci-fi spy novels that bend the old conventions of tradecraft and counterintelligence in fantastically original directions.

Nonetheless, in the future as in the past, what will astound readers of real-life spy stories in the press, and devotees of the spy in fiction, is the extent to which the reality of espionage outpaces the creativity of the spy novelist in the bizarre, unexpected, and quite unique ways in which the behavior of human spies unfolds. In the spy world, truth *is* often stranger than fiction. We know enough now about the case of Robert P. Hanssen, for example, to say amen to that observation.

Finally, another truth is also inescapable. As long as there is human interaction on this planet, there will always be spies. Somerset Maugham put it well in 1927:

> But there will always be espionage and there will always be counter-espionage. Though conditions may have altered, though difficulties may be greater, when war is raging, there will always be secrets which one side jealously guards and which the other will use every means to discover; there will always be men who from malice or for money will betray their kith and kin and there will always be men who, from love of adventure or a sense of duty, will risk a shameful death to secure information valuable to their country.[3]

Epilogue

And ye shall know the truth, and the truth
shall make you free.

John 8:32

This verse from the gospel writer John's account of
Christ's lesson to the Jews, scribes, and Pharisees on the Mount
of Olives was said to have been a favorite of DCI Allen Dulles,
a Presbyterian clergyman's son, who was principally responsible for the construction of the original CIA headquarters building in Langley, Virginia. In any event, these thirteen words
adorn the spacious entry foyer of that building, across from the
wall of honor on which the names of the intelligence officers
who died in service to their country are engraved.

It strikes me that this biblical injunction is a good starting
point for unraveling the mystery I set for the reader at the outset of this work: Is the truth of espionage stranger than the spy
fiction?

I would argue that in the technical world of espionage, the
real genius of human inventiveness and creativity exceeds the
imagination of Ian Fleming or Tom Clancy, even on a bad day.
In the rarefied world of cryptanalysis, what was accomplished
by U.S. Army and Navy code breakers prior to World War II in
cracking the Japanese diplomatic code, the success of the

British at Bletchley Park on Ultra; and the joint U.S.-British effort called VENONA to read Soviet diplomatic traffic after 1943 are stupefying achievements of patience and persistence in the face of mind-numbing repetitions of numerical analysis in search of patterns, in an age before computer assistance.

Moreover, the unprecedented lash-up of government, business, and academia that produced the U-2 spy plane in the 1950s and followed it with the Corona, KH-11, and RHYOLITE overhead reconnaissance and SIGINT collection systems is unique and beyond the ken of most spy fiction writers. These intelligence collection platforms have become so sophisticated now that not only do policy makers in Washington have real-time access to their product but so do tank drivers on the field of battle. Equally astonishing has been the recent development of the Predator unmanned aerial vehicle that has been used recently to track Taliban fugitives in the Tora Bora mountains of eastern Afghanistan and also destroy Al Qaeda operatives with missile firings on the ground in Yemen.

I would further argue that the more down-to-earth espionage escapades of the early Cold War such as the Berlin Tunnel and its counterpart in Vienna; the brash boldness of the *Glomar Explorer* effort to raise a submerged Soviet sub; and the compromised tunnel into the new Russian embassy on Mt. Alto in Washington are evidence of a real spy mind-set that does not fear physical or technical limits. Western spymasters in particular believed that with the patient application of brains, time, and money almost any technical obstacle to intelligence gathering against their adversaries could be surmounted. And when it could not, as in the case of trying to invade Cuba with too few assault troops in the wrong place with inadequate air cover, the cause was not an absence of know-how or means, but the blind and unrealistic maintenance of an ideal of "plausible deniability" in circumstances where the principle could not be maintained.

In my judgment, however, the human side of espionage is more peculiar than the fictional accounts portray it, for a different reason. It is not that the spy novelist cannot outdo the real thing in terms of raw creativity, it is that no writer is capable of imagining *all* the ways in which a human spy can scheme, rationalize, justify, and alter his behavior to perform his espionage mission.

Consider the actions of Oleg Penkovsky, Pyotr Popov, Aldrich Ames, and Robert Hanssen, the real-life spies we have looked at in this work, and attempt to diagram their psychological underpinnings, discern their real motives for spying, or describe their peculiar rationalizations/justifications for what they did. You would have a tough assignment. Penkovsky's betrayal of his inner-circle position in the hierarchy of Soviet military intelligence is difficult to explain fully by the frustrations he encountered to his promotion to general officer or his admiration for U.S. Army Colonel Peeke. Popov's operational carelessness in bringing out hard-to-conceal documents from Soviet military command headquarters in Vienna and his reckless willingness to identify himself to allied military strangers manifested a kind of insensitivity to the risks he was running that approached a death wish. Aldrich Ames spent his spy salary from the Soviets like a drunken sailor on home leave. Like Popov and Penkovsky, he must have indulged in such a narcissistic fantasy of his own extraordinary ability to avoid detection, or such disregard for the counterintelligence capabilities of his own service, that he was willing to take large and unnecessary risks of being found out. Finally, the Robert Hanssen who never met personally with his Soviet handlers and dictated the terms of his cooperation with them risked it all in the kinky pursuit of a luckless stripper in Washington, D.C.

What this all adds up to for me is that espionage is a vastly more complicated enterprise for human beings than even the coldest, cleverest, most calculating traitor can imagine. In the doing of it, spies get put into situations they never foresaw and undergo pressures they never dreamed of, and the necessity of living a lonely double or triple life quite simply wears them down. Nobody ever wrote that betraying one's family, friends, coworkers, and countrymen would be easy. As a consequence, there are very few human spies who can do it for a lifetime. The ideological spies had the best record, but many of them became careless in the end. Thus, I feel confident in maintaining that few spy novelists can capture the full range of human emotions and pressures that the life of a spy entails. The snowflake has too many crystals. With the exception perhaps of the fictional Magnus Pym—and he of course bolted after his father's death—the protagonists in the spy fiction I am most familiar with pale in comparison to their real-life counterparts. They are not nearly as complex in character or bizarre in behavior as the real thing.

The spy fiction that we have considered in this book is as compellingly good literature on any subject as has been written. Nevertheless, the truth that makes you free in the real world of espionage is that no fictional account adequately captures the remarkable variety of twists and turns that a genuine human spy goes through in pursuit of his mission of treachery and betrayal.

Notes

Introduction

1. Rudyard Kipling, *Kim* (1901; New York: Bantam Classics, 1983), pp. 116, 144–145, 181, 200.
2. Kim Philby, *My Silent War* (New York: Grove Press, 1968), p. 49.
3. Sherman Kent, *Strategic Intelligence for American World Policy* (Princeton: Princeton University Press, 1949), p. 6.

One: Recruitment

1. Duane R. Clarridge, *A Spy for All Seasons: My Life in the CIA* (New York: Scribner, 1997), p. 81.
2. David Ignatius, *Agents of Innocence* (New York: Norton, 1987), pp. 90–91.
3. Ibid., p. 211.
4. Clarridge, *A Spy for All Seasons*, p. 93.
5. Ibid., p. 77.
6. John le Carré, *Tinker, Tailor, Soldier, Spy* (New York: Knopf, 1974), p. 195.
7. Ibid., pp. 205–206.
8. John le Carré, *A Perfect Spy* (New York: Knopf, 1986), p. 255.
9. John Banville, *The Untouchable* (London: Picador, 1977).
10. Ibid., pp. 22, 47.
11. Ibid., pp. 104, 112.
12. Miranda Carter, *Anthony Blunt: His Lives* (New York: Farrar, Straus & Giroux, 2001), pp. 269–272.
13. Clarridge, *A Spy for All Seasons*, p. 124.
14. Graham Greene, *The Human Factor* (New York: Simon & Schuster, 1978), pp. 140–141.

Two: Betrayal

1. Le Carré, *A Perfect Spy,* p. 121.
2. Carter, *Anthony Blunt,* p. 272.
3. Alan Studner, quoted in Jerrold L. Schecter and Peter S. Deriabin, *The Spy Who Saved the World: How a Soviet Colonel Changed the Course of the Cold War* (New York: Scribner's, 1992), p. 389.
4. Alan Studner, quoted in ibid., p. 390.
5. Philby, *My Silent War,* p. xvi.
6. Ibid., p. xix.
7. Graham Greene, *The Confidential Agent,* quoted in Philby, *My Silent War,* p. xx.
8. Le Carré, *Tinker, Tailor, Soldier, Spy,* p. 332.
9. Le Carré, *A Perfect Spy,* pp. 97–98.
10. Ibid., p. 276.
11. Ibid., p. 432.
12. Ibid., p. 471.
13. Quoted in John G. Cawelti and Bruce A. Rosenberg, *The Spy Story* (Chicago: University of Chicago Press, 1987), p. 120.

Three: The Spy Bureaucracy

1. W. Somerset Maugham, *Ashenden; or: The British Agent* (1928; New York: Doubleday, Doran, 1941), pp. 4, 7.
2. John le Carré, *The Spy Who Came In from the Cold* (1963; New York: Ballantine Books, 1992).
3. Ibid., p. 239.
4. Christopher Andrew, *For the President's Eyes Only: Secret Intelligence and the American Presidency from Washington to Bush* (1995; New York: Harper Perennial, 1996); p. 261.
5. Ignatius, *Agents of Innocence,* pp. 369–370.
6. Ibid., pp. 441–442.
7. Robert Baer, *See No Evil: The True Story of a Ground Soldier in the CIA's War on Terrorism* (New York: Crown, 2002).
8. Clarridge, *A Spy for All Seasons,* p. 294.
9. Greene, *The Human Factor,* p. 215.

Four: Counterintelligence

1. Le Carré, *Tinker, Tailor, Soldier, Spy,* pp. 17–18.
2. Ibid., pp. 319–320.
3. Ibid., p. 73.
4. Ibid., p. 292.
5. Ignatius, *Agents of Innocence,* pp. 440–441.

6. Paul Redmond, speech to Central Intelligence Retirees Association (CIRA), Washington, D.C., February 4, 2002.

Five: Tradecraft

1. Le Carré, *Tinker, Tailor, Soldier, Spy,* p. 328.
2. Ibid., p. 276.
3. Frederick Forsyth, *The Day of the Jackal* (New York: Viking Press, 1971).
4. Le Carré, *A Perfect Spy,* p. 252.
5. Joseph Conrad, *The Secret Agent* (1907; New York: Knopf, 1962).
6. Le Carré, *Tinker, Tailor, Soldier, Spy,* pp. 315, 353.

Six: Heroes

1. Conrad, *The Secret Agent,* p. 217.
2. Ibid., p. 26.
3. Ibid., p. 216.
4. Ibid., p. 162.
5. Erskine Childers, *The Riddle of the Sands* (1903; London: Penguin, 1952), p. 108.
6. Ibid., p. 121.
7. Ibid., p. 257.
8. John A. Buchan, *The Thirty-nine Steps* (1915; Boston: Godine, 1991), p. 62.
9. Ibid., p. 105.
10. Clarridge, *A Spy for All Seasons,* p. 76.
11. William Hood, *Mole* (New York: Norton, 1982), p. 206.
12. David E. Murphy, Sergei Kondrashev, and George Bailey, *Battleground Berlin: CIA vs. KGB in the Cold War* (New Haven: Yale University Press, 1997).
13. Tom Clancy, *The Hunt for Red October* (Annapolis, Md.: Naval Institute Press, 1984), pp. 25–26.
14. Ibid., p. 34.
15. Ibid., p. 35.
16. Schecter and Deriabin, *The Spy Who Saved the World,* pp. 92–93.

Seven: Spies and Sex

1. Ian Fleming, *From Russia, With Love* (1957; New York: MJF Books, 1996), p. 88.
2. Le Carré, *Tinker, Tailor, Soldier, Spy,* p. 350.
3. David Wise, *Spy: The Inside Story of How the FBI's Robert Hanssen Betrayed America* (New York: Random House, 2002), pp. 111–112.

Eight: Assassination

1. Maugham, *Ashenden,* pp. 244–245.
2. Forsyth, *The Day of the Jackal,* pp. 44–45.
3. Nicholas D. Kristof, "The Osirak Option," *New York Times,* November 15, 2002, p. A27.
4. Charles McCarry, *The Tears of Autumn: A Novel* (New York: Dutton, 1975).
5. Ibid., p. 132.
6. Ronald L. Goldfarb, *Perfect Villains, Imperfect Heroes: Robert F. Kennedy's War Against Organized Crime* (New York: Random House, 1995), p. 258 ff.
7. Alan Furst, *Dark Star* (New York: Random House, 1991).

Nine: Villains and Fabricators

1. Greene, *The Human Factor,* pp. 130, 136.
2. Forsyth, *The Day of the Jackal,* pp. 44–45.
3. Ibid., p. 50.
4. Banville, *The Untouchable,* pp. 21–22.
5. Le Carré, *A Perfect Spy,* p. 381.
6. Maugham, *Ashenden,* p. 154.

Ten: Sci-Fi

1. Jeffrey T. Richelson, *The Wizards of Langley: Inside the CIA's Directorate of Science and Technology* (Boulder, Colo.: Westview Press, 2001).

Eleven: The Game for the Sake of the Game

1. Kipling, *Kim,* pp. 2–3.
2. Greene, *The Human Factor,* p. 339.
3. Le Carré, *The Spy Who Came In from the Cold,* pp. 17–18.
4. Le Carré, *Tinker, Tailor, Soldier, Spy,* pp. 331–332.
5. Clarridge, *A Spy for All Seasons,* p. 412.
6. Philby, *My Silent War,* p. 90.
7. David A. Vise, *The Bureau and the Mole: The Unmasking of Robert Philip Hanssen, the Most Dangerous Spy in U.S. History* (New York: Atlantic Monthly Press, 2002).
8. Robert P. Hanssen message, quoted in Vise, *The Bureau and the Mole,* p. 201.
9. Hanssen, quoted in ibid., p. 216.

10. David Charney, interviewed by the author, July 10, 2002.
11. Hanssen, quoted in Vise, *The Bureau and the Mole*, p. 225.

Twelve: Spying on Friends and Allies

1. *British Security Coordination: The Secret History of British Intelligence in the Americas, 1940–1945* (New York: Fromm International, 1999).

Thirteen: Terrorism and Intelligence

1. John le Carré, *The Russia House* (New York: Knopf, 1989), p. 208.
2. Ibid., p. 209.
3. Ian Fleming, *Goldfinger* (1959), in *A James Bond Omnibus*, vol. 1 (New York: MJF Books, 1996), p. 204.

Fourteen: The Rogue Elephant

1. John Lewis Gaddis, *We Now Know* (New York: Oxford University Press, 1997).
2. Robert Littell, *The Company: A Novel of the CIA* (New York: Overlook Press, 2002), p. 649.

Fifteen: Life After Spying

1. Ambler, Eric. *A Coffin for Dimitrios* (1939; New York: Carroll & Graf, 1996), p. 52.
2. Le Carré, *The Russia House*, p. 85.

Conclusion: Myth or Reality—Does Espionage Have a Future?

1. Maugham, *Ashenden*, p. x.
2. National Security Act of 1947.
3. Ibid., pp. xii–xiii.

Acknowledgments

I should like to acknowledge my indebtedness to my literary agent, Ron Goldfarb, for pressing me to write this book. I had come to him originally with a scheme to produce yet another "What's wrong with American intelligence" tome, which would doubtless have taken its place with all the others, gathering dust on library shelves. My editor at Knopf, Pat Hass, has been stalwart in keeping me on task, with good feedback and ample encouragement. Professor Wesley Wark at the University of Toronto was the person who originally encouraged me to give a course on the spy novel and suggested several of the titles I came to admire most. Finally, it was Hank Dobin, associate dean of the College at Princeton who suggested the juxtaposition of myth and reality in espionage as an appropriate theme for a freshman seminar that started me thinking about this subject. I am much in the debt of all four in these different ways.

Index

References to illustrations are in *italics;* references to fictional characters use quotation marks.

Permissions Acknowledgments

Grateful acknowledgment is made to the following for permission to reprint previously published material:

Alfred A. Knopf: Excerpts from *A Cabin for Dimitrios* by Eric Ambler. Copyright © 1939 and renewed 1967 by Eric Ambler. Excerpts from *Russia House* by John le Carré. Copyright © 1989 by John le Carré. Reprinted by permission of Alfred A. Knopf, a division of Random House, Inc.

Brassey's, Inc.: Excerpts from *Mole* by William Hood. Reprinted by permission of Brassey's, Inc.

David Higham Associates: Excerpts from *The Spy Who Came In from the Cold; Tinker Tailor, Soldier, Spy; A Perfect Spy* by John le Carré (Pocket Books, New York). Reprinted by permission of David Higham Associates on behalf of the author.

Doubleday: Excerpts from *Ashenden or the British Agent* by W. Somerset Maugham. Reprinted by permission of Doubleday, a division of Random House, Inc.

Grove/Atlantic Inc.: Excerpts from *The Bureau and the Mole* by David Vise. Reprinted by permission of Grove/Atlantic, Inc.

Ian Fleming Publications Ltd.: Excerpt from *Goldfinger* by Ian Fleming. Copyright © 1959 by Glidrose Productions Ltd. Reprinted by permission of Ian Fleming Publications Ltd.

Leona P. Schecter Literary Agency: Excerpts from *The Spy Who Saved the World* by Jarrold Schecter and Peter Deriabin. Reprinted by permission of the Leona P. Schecter Literary Agency.

Naval Institute Press: Excerpts from *The Hunt for Red October* by Tom Clancy. Copyright © 1984 by U.S. Naval Institute. Excerpts from *The Riddle of the Sands* by Erskine Childers. Reprinted by permission of the Naval Institute Press.

The Overlook Press: Excerpts from *The Company* by Robert Littell. Copyright © 2002 by Robert Littell. Reprinted by permission of The Overlook Press.

Photographic Credits

Grateful acknowledgment is made to the following for permission to reprint illustrations appearing on the pages indicated:

AP/Wide World Photos: 31
CIA: 92
CIA and NCIC: 148
Doubleday and Co.: 139, 172
The Image Works: 121
David Murphy and Yale University Press: 68
Photofest: 17, 43
Cassi Trowbridge: 15

A Note About the Author

FREDERICK P. HITZ teaches at the Woodrow Wilson School of Princeton University. He is a graduate of Princeton and the Harvard Law School and spent more than twenty years in the federal government, most of it at the CIA, where from 1990 to 1998 he was the first presidentially appointed inspector general.

A Note on the Type

This book was set in New Caledonia, the digitized version of a Linotype face designed by W. A. Dwiggins (1880–1956). It belongs to the family of printing types called "modern face" by printers—a term used to mark the change in style of the type letters that occurred around 1800.

Composed by North Market Street Graphics,
Lancaster, Pennsylvania
Printed and bound by R. R. Donnelley & Sons,
Harrisonburg, Virginia
Designed by Anthea Lingeman